GW00568812

Built to Innovate shows how leaders can create an innovating engine that mobilizes all the people who work for their organization. The book offers both a big-picture conceptual framework and a proven method developed through many years of academic research and practice. It is filled with interesting examples and is thought provoking. It is a must-read.

—W. Chan Kim, BCG Chair Professor of INSEAD and World's #1 Management Thinker by Thinkers50

In today's world, a company that does not innovate cannot succeed. In the best organizations, everyone from the C-suite to the factory floor is enabled and encouraged to innovate. Fortunately, there are tools and systems that can be used to stimulate innovation in any industry, and Ben M. Bensaou's new book is comprehensive and remarkable in this respect.

—Güler Sabancı, Chair, Sabancı Holding

Innovation is a core challenge for all leaders, and I am focused on it as governor of Japan's No. 1 industrial center, which is aiming to shape the world's foremost and unparalleled startups ecosystem. Ben M. Bensaou's *Built to Innovate* offers insights into the why, the how, and the who of innovating that leaders in business, the nonprofit sector, and government alike are sure to find compelling and powerful.

—Hideaki Ohmura, Governor, Aichi Prefecture, Japan

In an era when tech rules the markets, everyone will advise you to innovate more. Yet no one ever tells you *how* to do this. Ben M. Bensaou provides an immensely valuable, nuanced set of approaches to enhance innovating as a truly organizational process. This is a must-read for anyone tasked with ramping up their company's innovating engine.

—Toby Stuart, Helzel Professor of Entrepreneurship, Strategy, and Innovation; Associate Dean, External Affairs; and Faculty Director, Institute for Business Innovation, Haas School of Business, UC Berkeley

Innovating should be everyone's habit, but it's usually done by a select few. Bensaou's BTI framework and his seven-step process show how everyone can participate in priming the organization's innovating engine to forge a pathway to a profitable future.

—N. Venkat Venkatraman, author of *The Digital Matrix* and David J. McGrath Jr. Professor of Management, Boston University, Questrom School of Business

With fresh eyes, Ben M. Bensaou peers backstage into some of the world's most innovative companies to reveal a number of elegant and original concepts and tools. His carefully crafted stories and well-researched cases will teach leaders how to create a culture of innovation and reward anyone interested in the science and practice of innovating.

—Dr. Jon Arsen Chilingerian, PhD, Professor of Health Care Management, Heller School at Brandeis University, and Director of the MD/MBA and EMBA Physician Programs, Tufts University School of Medicine

BUILT TO INNOVATE

BUILT TO INNOVATE

ESSENTIAL PRACTICES
TO WIRE INNOVATION INTO
YOUR COMPANY'S DNA

BEN M. BENSAOU
with Karl Weber

New York Chicago San Francisco Athens London Madrid
Mexico City Milan New Delhi Singapore Sydney Toronto

1 2 3 4 5 6 7 8 9   LCR   26 25 24 23 22 21

ISBN   978-1-260-46269-2
MHID   1-260-46269-2

e-ISBN   978-1-260-46270-8
e-MHID   1-260-46270-6

Library of Congress Cataloging-in-Publication Data

Names: Bensaou, Ben M., author.
Title: Built to innovate : essential practices to wire innovation into your company's DNA / Ben M. Bensaou, with Karl Weber.
Description: New York : McGraw Hill Education, [2022] | Includes bibliographical references and index.
Identifiers: LCCN 2021019654 (print) | LCCN 2021019655 (ebook) | ISBN 9781260462692 (hardback) | ISBN 9781260462708 (ebook)
Subjects: LCSH: Creative ability in business—Management. | Technological innovations—Management. | Diffusion of innovations—Management. | Organizational change.
Classification: LCC HD53 .B4385 2022 (print) | LCC HD53 (ebook) | DDC 658.4/063—dc23
LC record available at https://lccn.loc.gov/2021019654
LC ebook record available at https://lccn.loc.gov/2021019655

McGraw Hill books are available at special quantity discounts to use as premiums and sales promotions or for use in corporate training programs. To contact a representative, please visit the Contact Us pages at www.mhprofessional.com.

For my father

CONTENTS

PART THREE

The Three Key Roles in Innovating

PART FOUR

The Infrastructure for Innovating
Governance and Coordination

INTRODUCTION

Why a New Book on Innovation?

In a world where technological, economic, and social changes from political upheavals to devastating pandemics seem to be increasingly rapid and unpredictable . . . where unanticipated sources of competitive pressure are continually arising . . . where complicated global forces are constantly reshaping markets . . . and where the effective life spans of successful product and service offerings seem to be steadily shrinking—in such a world, leaders of organizations in every sector and industry are desperately in search of the secret of innovation. "What worked for us last year won't work tomorrow" is their lament. "We need to find a new and better way—and we need to find it *now*, before our rivals across town or across the planet find it."

We live in a time when change is the rule, not the exception. And this means that organizations (whether for-profit companies, nonprofit organizations, or government agencies) must constantly succeed at two very different, even contradictory activities. They must be exceedingly good at doing what they do today—at providing customers with the goods or services they have come to expect, and doing so with superlative quality, efficiency, convenience, affordability, and style. This is the challenge of *execution*, which leaders in every type of organization spend a lifetime mastering.

Yet these same leaders must simultaneously excel at rethinking, reimagining, and improving what they do today, finding ways to improve their current products and processes as well as devising entirely new ones that no one has yet envisioned. This is the challenge of *innovating.*

The Twin Engines That Drive Your Organization

Thus, every organization needs to operate through both an *execution engine* and an *innovating engine.*

Execution, of course, is tremendously important. Business schools, consultants and trainers, scholars of business, and authors of business books devote lots of time and energy to studying, analyzing, and teaching execution methods for all sorts of processes that take place in organizations of every kind—planning, research, finance, manufacturing, sales, marketing, logistics, human resources, and many more. Detailed, practical, well-designed systems for executing these processes have been developed and adopted by organizations, and countless employees have been trained in carrying out these systems. And day in, day out, the vast majority of employees in organizations devote almost all of their time to execution. That's understandable, since virtually all systems for training, leading, managing, incentivizing, and evaluating employees focus almost exclusively on execution. In fact, if we could see inside the mind of the typical corporate worker and analyze what that worker devotes his or her days to thinking about, we might conclude that execution is the *only* thing that businesses exist to do.

This book is about the other crucial organizational engine—the innovating engine. It explains how to embed and nurture innovating capabilities, thereby building the organization's innovating engine. This can be done through the essential practices I will describe in this book.

Notice the subtle distinction I draw between the words *innovation* and *innovating. Innovation* refers to the output of innovating—a product, a technology, a service, and a process. Innovation as output tends to be associated with an individual genius, a research and development specialist, a great designer, or a business model creator.

By contrast, *innovating* refers to a process. I define it as follows:

> Innovating is systematically looking for, developing, and implementing new ideas that create value for a customer and for the organization.

Notice that, as defined, the concept of *innovating* carries with it several important implications:

- ▸ Innovating is something that everyone in an organization can do.
- ▸ *Systematically* means both continuously and using a system—that is, a structured method.
- ▸ Innovating begins with *looking for* ideas—not necessarily finding them. (After all, we can control the act of looking; we can't control the act of finding.) Hence the importance of encouraging everyone to keep looking, anytime and anywhere.
- ▸ A *new idea* is one that is new to your organization, even if it already exists in another industry or company.
- ▸ The term *customer* should be defined as broadly as possible. It should include anyone you serve, whether this is based on the purchase of a product or service or on some form of nonfinancial exchange. A customer may also be outside or inside the organization; for example, the customers of an organization's human resources department include staff members, managers, and top executives within the organization.
- ▸ Innovating is a habit to be practiced at all times—you can innovate in everything you do.

Most employees devote little time or energy to thinking about their role in the innovating engine. This is not to say that the concept of innovation is one that business thinkers ignore. In fact, bookstore shelves groan under the weight of titles that promise to provide the "secret sauce" that will let your organization become more creative, vibrant, and innovative. Many of these books have some useful insights as well as colorful stories that illustrate how particular companies have earned their reputations as hothouses of innovation—for example, firms like Apple, Amazon, 3M, Google, and Facebook.

The stories of innovative breakthroughs by companies in such "creative" fields as high technology and entertainment are colorful and inspiring—but by themselves they generally fail to provide business leaders with concrete guidance as to what they can *do* to make their organizations more innovative. Few of these books grapple concretely with the realities of building and running an innovating engine. Most fail to recognize that *the entire organization,* including all the people who work for it, has a role to play in the innovating engine. As a result, they don't provide a systematic process that can be used to make the innovating engine hum.

As I searched the literature for a book I could recommend to the business leaders who've asked me for help with innovation, I was unable to find one with the combination of features that organizations most need:

- A set of clear, simple innovating processes that companies can use to generate valuable improvements and changes in every aspect of their work
- Principles of innovating that can help companies produce and implement not just new product ideas but also process improvements, customer service enhancements, new business models, and more
- An explanation of how everyone in an organization, from frontline employees to midlevel managers to senior

leaders, can and must contribute to innovating, with specific guidance for team members at all of these levels

▶ A detailed, concrete explanation of the role of dedicated innovation specialists—what I call the I-Team—in jump-starting the work of innovating throughout the organization, including descriptions of how successful companies have created, organized, and implemented such a team

▶ A methodology with a kit of proven processes and tools that companies in any industry can use to generate innovative ideas that will bring new value to customers both inside and outside the organization

▶ Illustrative examples and cases drawn not just from the familiar superstars of innovation—especially those from industries like high-tech, consumer products, and entertainment—but from lesser-known companies in industries and markets most people don't associate with innovation

More than 20 years ago, I set out to remedy this problem. Since then, my research, coaching, teaching, and consulting work with dozens of companies around the world has provided me with the insights, observations, stories, and systems needed to fill these gaps in our understanding of how to make innovation work. I've been developing and testing tools and concepts for promoting innovation, training managers at every level in how to use these tools, studying the results achieved, and using those observations to refine my thinking. The result has been an approach to innovation that many companies have found particularly powerful in helping them enhance their organizations' innovative capacity. I believe the set of ideas, tools, and stories presented in this book can do the same for you.

Many organizations are now discovering that it's possible to consciously develop and implement a rational, step-by-step system for innovating that helps to ensure a steady stream of new ideas and product or process improvements. In this book, I'll recount my experiences in researching and working with some of these organizations. They include an international array of companies like BASF, AkzoNobel, Allianz, Bayer, W. L. Gore, Kordsa, Ecocem, Fiskars, Samsung, Recruit Holdings, Marvel Studios, Domino's Pizza, and Starwood, operating in industries ranging from electronics, chemicals, and building materials to insurance, moviemaking, and hospitality. These companies are demonstrating that innovating can become a habit—one that provides an organization with a powerful advantage over its rivals in the marketplace. And nonprofit organizations and governmental agencies from around the world are also following suit, bringing innovative excellence to arenas long viewed as hidebound and incapable of change.

In the chapters that follow, I'll describe in detail the roles that employees at every level of your organization need to play in implementing this system, from frontline workers to mid-level managers to the executives in the C-suite. I'll show that innovating needs to be not just a "top-down" process driven by mandates from on high, but also a "bottom-up" and "middle-out" process driven by empowered leaders in every department. I'll explain how members of the I-Team— trained to encourage innovation, to surface the best new ideas, and to channel them to the parts of the organization where they can grow best—can be integrated into every department of your company. And I'll show how leaders at every level of your business can use the various tools and process methodologies in my innovating kit to stimulate fresh thinking and generate the ideas you need to grow and thrive.

The Three Key Processes of Innovating

Many books offer tools and techniques for creativity. I'll refer to these on occasion. But my central purpose in this book is to provide leaders with a conceptual framework that can guide them in designing and continually nurturing an organization built to innovate. This framework will suggest important new ways of thinking about the roles of frontline employees, middle managers, and senior executives in an organization, as well as the ways these groups of individuals interact with one another.

Your company's innovating engine is driven by three key processes of innovating: *creation, integration,* and *reframing.* To build your innovating engine—which will operate in parallel with your existing execution engine—everyone within the company must be engaged in these three processes in addition to his or her existing execution engine role.

Creation is the process by which the organization continuously generates new ideas—the raw materials of innovating. These new ideas can relate to practically any activity that the organization performs. For example, they can include ideas for new or improved products or services that customers may like; ideas for identifying and serving new customers or markets; ideas for making the processes for manufacturing products or delivering services faster, more efficient, safer, or more reliable; ideas for making it easier for employees to capture, process, and share information; or any other kind of idea with the potential to improve an organization's operations. When an organization has built an innovating engine, it innovates in everything it does—in technology, products, and services, as well as in management processes and internal functions. And that means the process of creation is constantly happening in every department and division of the organization.

Integration is the second process in the innovating system. This is the process by which the dispersed innovating capabilities and resources within the firm are brought together into a corporatewide innovating capability. You can think of integration as the process by which the organization "connects the dots" among all the ideas springing from the frontline employees as well as other levels of the organization. The integration process connects people, linking innovators throughout the company into a social network fully dedicated to innovating. The connecting network may also extend beyond the boundaries of the organization, including external innovation partners such as customers, suppliers, startup companies, academic institutions, and more.

At great innovating companies, the integration process includes a system for evaluating, selecting, supporting, and channeling the best ideas that emerge from the creation process. I'll discuss how your organization can build a companywide system dedicated to making innovating an everyday reality.

Reframing is the third process of innovating. To prepare for the future, every organization has to keep questioning its existing strategy even while implementing it. Continually challenging the accepted dogma, conventional orthodoxies, and underlying assumptions on which your current execution-space activities are based is essential to making change and progress possible. But this is very hard to do during your ordinary daily activities. When you're immersed in execution, you are so focused on following standard procedures as efficiently as possible that it's almost impossible to achieve the psychological distance needed to see the possible weaknesses or gaps in those procedures.

The process of reframing offers a solution. When you pause in your execution work to evaluate the effectiveness of an innovative idea, you suddenly have a new benchmark by which to measure the value of your current processes. Comparing old and new ideas makes it easier to recognize the fact that your familiar ways of viewing the world and your work are not the only ways—and to see that change is possible and may even be desirable.

Reframing, then, is about shifting your mental gears sufficiently to recognize the potential value in an innovation. It's also about altering your assumptions about your business so as to make the innovation part of a new status quo—a better way of working that creates more value for you and for your customers.

People at every level within the organization all have distinctive contributions to make to each of these three innovating processes. In describing their roles as part of the innovating engine, I refer to the three main levels of the organization as *frontline innovators, midlevel coaches,* and *senior leaders.*

My study of how innovation-centered companies operate has helped me to develop the Built to Innovate (BTI) Framework, illustrated in Figure I.1.[1]

	Frontline Innovators	Midlevel Coaches	Senior Leaders
Reframing	Look Beyond the Obvious	Give Permission to Innovate; Create a Fair Process	Put Innovation at the Core of Strategy; Allow Challenges to Assumptions
Integration	Share Innovative Practices and Customer Knowledge	Build a Connective Process; Link the Execution and Innovating Engines	Create a Governance Structure and a Language for Innovating
Creation	Generate Ideas by Listening to Customers and Noncustomers	Provide Support; Review and Channel Ideas	Set Norms, Standards, and Incentives for Innovating

FIGURE I.1 The BTI Framework

Innovation by Anyone, Anytime, Anywhere—How the Three Processes of Innovating Take Place at Three Levels of an Organization

As Figure I.1 illustrates, all three processes—creation, integration, and reframing—should be taking place at any given time in each of the three major levels in most organizations. All three levels have important roles to play in each of the three innovating processes, although different groups are likely to take the lead on specific processes in particular circumstances.

Note that, in this illustration, the lines separating the three organizational levels, as well as the lines dividing the three processes from one another, are dotted lines rather than solid ones. This reflects the fact that, in the real world, the distinctions among hierarchical levels are often porous and shifting rather than rigid and fixed, as well as the fact that the innovating activities of creation, integration, and reframing are closely interconnected and overlap to some degree.

Also note that the BTI framework does *not* assume the traditional top-down approach to innovating. Instead, the building of an innovating engine can begin anywhere. It can start with frontline innovators who generate ideas, design experiments, develop prototypes, and showcase their successes. My motto for this model of innovation is "Don't ask for permission—make others jealous!" Once frontline innovators in a single department have shown the way with a handful of successful breakthroughs, others throughout the company will be eager to imitate them.

Innovating can also start with senior leaders who take steps to eliminate obstacles, encourage innovating behaviors, and communicate that innovating is part of everyone's job—the starting point to the reframing process. Or it can start with midlevel coaches, who launch the innovating process by offering their frontline employees training, guidance, support, and connections to resources from elsewhere in the firm.

Your ultimate goal should be to build a complete innovating engine that embeds all three processes at each level of your organization. But this takes time. The good news is that you don't need to wait until the process is completed to harvest the fruits of innovation. No matter how and where innovating first emerges in your company, you can begin reaping the benefits almost immediately.

Traits of an Organization Built to Innovate

The first core trait of an organization built to innovate is its ability to inspire individual creativity and initiative in all its people. In this book, I will illustrate how companies like Bayer, Gore, Kordsa, and Starwood have developed this ability, and I will draw some general lessons from their organizational and management practices to suggest how others may learn from them.

The second core trait of an organization built to innovate is its ability to link and leverage the distributed pockets of innovating activity and individual expertise across the organization by connecting frontline innovators into a coordinated community and an integrated process of organizational learning. I will describe how everyone contributes to this integrating process, drawing on my observations from companies around the world, including Fiskars, Allianz, and Recruit Holdings.

The third core trait in my conceptual model for the innovating engine is an organization's ability to continuously question itself and challenge some of its shared assumptions about its business and customers. I will provide a number of examples of companies that have been able to develop such a capability, such as BASF and Marvel Studios. And while it is clear that the actual methods, tools, and processes for carrying on the transformation task will be different for different companies and adapted to the unique situations of each company, it is also equally clear that the kind of outcomes these companies have achieved are attainable by others.

Thus, the kind of "collective genius" that is widely admired in companies such as Apple, Amazon, and Pixar is not restricted to organizations led by brilliant individual leaders like Steve Jobs or Jeff Bezos.[2] It can also emerge through the use of systematic processes that draw together the contributions of countless individuals, none of them considered an outstanding "genius" yet all of them capable of participating constructively in the organizationwide process of innovating.

The Structure of the Book

Built to Innovate is divided into four parts. In Part One, "The Innovating Habit," I'll present my overall approach to innovating;

I'll explain why innovating is an activity that everyone in your organization should participate in; I'll sketch the special characteristics and distinguishing features of the twin "engines" every organization should have—the execution engine and the innovating engine; and I'll explain why the most important element of the innovating engine is the shift from the supplier-side view to the customer-side view.

In Part Two, "The Three Key Processes of Innovating," I'll describe the processes of creation, integration, and reframing, each of which is essential to the practice of innovating. I'll also show how employees at every level of the organization, including frontline workers, midlevel managers, and senior leaders, need to be involved in all of these processes.

Part Three, "The Three Key Roles in Innovating," delves more deeply into each of the three organizational levels, exploring in some detail the particular roles that employees at each of these levels should play in carrying out the three key processes of innovating.

Finally, Part Four, "The Infrastructure for Innovating Governance and Coordination," offers advice and guidance on designing and implementing an organizational structure that will enhance your company's ability to innovate successfully. Within Part Four, Chapter 10 is dedicated to offering a concrete process you can use to get the innovating habit started and to make it a routine part of your daily operations.

My hope is that, after reading this book, you'll be inspired to transform your own organization into an innovating organization, capable of continually producing new products and processes that generate enormous new value for you and for the customers you serve.

Now turn the page, and we'll get started.

PART ONE

THE INNOVATING HABIT

1

THE INNOVATING HABIT

JUMP-STARTING THE PRACTICE OF CREATIVITY

BASF is a German-based multinational that is the world's largest chemical company. Operating in more than 80 countries and employing over 117,000 people, BASF is involved in a wide range of businesses, including chemicals, plastics, agricultural products, oil and gas industry parts and equipment, and biotechnology. In 2019, the company's revenues exceeded €59 billion (almost $70 billion).

BASF also boasts a long history of innovation, from its role in developing the Haber-Bosch process (1913) for mass-producing fertilizer, which played a crucial role in dramatically increasing the world's food output, to its invention of the tape used in music cassettes (1935).[1] Today, it is working on technological breakthroughs that include safer, more eco-friendly plasticizer accelerators used in making products ranging from PVC piping to yoga mats; improved paints and coatings for automobile exteriors; innovative fragrances for use in perfumes, lotions, and shampoos; and new hybrid seeds that can greatly increase yields of basic crops like soy, corn, and cotton. In a typical year, BASF invests more than $2 billion in research and development (R&D), supports some 10,000 employees who are directly involved in product innovation, and generates 1,000 or more new patents—all figures that reflect the company's commitment to remaining one of the most innovative organizations in the chemical industry.

Given this stellar long-term track record, it might seem surprising that BASF would want to call on outside innovation consultants to help it improve its approach to innovation. But in the mid-2000s, though BASF's scientific track record was as strong as ever, that wasn't automatically translating into innovations that would produce value for BASF or its customers.

Meanwhile, structural changes were roiling the chemical industry. New competition was emerging from companies in Asia, where a pool of skilled, well-trained workers was becoming available at lower cost than in Europe or the United States, exerting downward price pressure on products like those made by BASF. Declining worldwide prices for petroleum, a core ingredient in many of the chemical products sold by BASF, were contributing to the price pressure. Under the circumstances, the company's leaders weren't content to assume that BASF's people would automatically make the mental and cultural shifts they needed to ensure that their approach to innovating would work for a new future. The company realized that a traditional approach to innovation, relying on the work of scientists and R&D specialists, was no longer sufficient. So BASF decided to build a more broadly based *innovating engine* to supplement its existing strengths in science and R&D.

Like many companies, BASF called on outside consultants with a special focus on innovation to help it with this new approach. The challenge was to help people throughout BASF find new ways to make innovating a part of their everyday work—thus creating future growth opportunities for a huge, successful company in a seemingly mature industrial space.

This wasn't an easy challenge to meet. But over the following decade, through the efforts of its own internal leadership and with advice from external innovation experts, BASF designed and implemented a cascading series of changes that affected every layer of the organization and every geographic and market division of its operations—all designed to infuse a new, more proactive, collaborative, and open-ended approach to innovation into the company's DNA. The result has been an accelerated and energized program of innovation that has helped BASF maintain its stature as the world's biggest chemical company, even under continuously increasing economic and competitive pressure.

I learned about BASF's remarkable innovation program in 2009 through one of the consultants who helped to shape it. He introduced me to Andrés Jaffé, the executive who guided the program during its early years. Jaffé invited me to visit with him and his team, launching a learning experience for me that has now spanned more than a decade.[2]

New Perspectives for a Venerable Company

The thousands of chemists, engineers, biologists, botanists, and other scientists and researchers who work at BASF have all the talent needed to maintain a steady flow of innovations. But talent alone doesn't produce innovations that serve customer needs and create value for both BASF and its various stakeholders. Equally essential is a deep understanding of customers and a readiness to collaborate with them in the process of generating ideas, developing and refining those ideas, and then executing them in an efficient, sustainable fashion. Nurturing such attitudes requires a particular kind of corporate culture—one that doesn't grow naturally or automatically in companies like BASF.

In fact, while opening up BASF to customer needs, problems, and insights might sound like a simple task, it was actually quite challenging. Most companies with a long history (BASF was founded in 1865) and a track record of success tend to develop an insular culture. Having shown themselves to be world-class experts in their fields of activity, company managers and employees begin to doubt that anyone outside their organizational walls has much to teach them. When the industry you work in is intensely competitive, the desire to safeguard your valuable intellectual property can easily lead to an emphasis on secrecy, which only increases the reluctance to engage in freewheeling discussions and explorations with outsiders—even when those outsiders are important company stakeholders.

BASF suffered to a degree from all these tendencies. As one observer noted, BASF was a company whose success had been driven "from the inside out: Excellence in research, driving innovation through proprietary labs, designing core processes with a focus on efficient manufacturing and product line optimization, flawless logistics, reliable delivery, and so on."[3]

All of these "inside-out" strengths are valuable and important. But BASF needed to develop a new set of "outside-in" capabilities that would enable the company and its people to learn from their customers and do a better job of keeping up with changes in the external environment.

BASF's leadership, up to and including the board of directors, recognized the problem. They launched a program, originally housed in the corporation's Marketing and Sales Academy, to foster interaction and dialogue with customers. Named "Help Our Customers to Be More Successful" (HCS), the project aimed at teaching BASF employees how to learn from customers without prejudging the results, to hold BASF's own solutions and approaches in abeyance rather than rushing to propose them to customers, and to value the diversity of customers and their needs rather than attempting to impose one-size-fits-all thinking on them.

The initial results of HCS were encouraging, suggesting to BASF that even greater value might be realized by making it available to a much broader range of corporate employees from departments extending far beyond marketing and sales, including product development, manufacturing, logistics, accounting, customer service, and more. As a result, HCS grew into a corporate culture change initiative called Perspectives. Led initially by Jacques Delmoitiez, president of BASF Polyurethanes, a successful $1.8 billion business, it was later taken over by his colleague, Andrés Jaffé. Its underlying goal was to establish a new enterprisewide focus on defining the unmet, often unstated needs of BASF's customers—as well as others not currently customers of the company—and on innovating to meet those needs. Jaffé's team included regional representatives from BASF businesses around the world as well as experts with particular forms of functional expertise, who could serve as internal business consultants for BASF units as they participated in the new initiative. As a focused internal entity dedicating to supporting innovation throughout the organization, Perspectives was BASF's first effort to systematically build its own innovating engine. Its overarching goal was to help increase the innovating capacity of BASF across the entire corporation.

Perspectives began with some deep analytical work into the nature of BASF's customer relationships. Within every business unit, cross-functional teams were created to meet with customers to discuss their needs, goals, and requirements. Studying the results and uncovering both the commonalities and the differences among BASF's thousands of customers enabled the teams to map those customers using a classification scheme made up of six different customer types, each demanding a different customer interaction model (CIM):

▸ *Type 1:* Customers who require products that meet standard specifications, for which price is typically the most important decision factor. In working with these customers, BASF acts as a Trader or Transactional Supplier.

▶ *Type 2:* Customers who require products that are of high quality and reliability, delivered on time. In working with these customers, BASF acts as a Lean or Reliable Basics Supplier.

▶ *Type 3:* Customers who want the freedom to mix and match standardized products and services to create their own packages for purchase. In working with these customers, BASF acts as a Standard Package Supplier.

▶ *Type 4:* Customers who require superior product performance, reflecting the latest innovations in the field. In working with these customers, BASF acts as a Product or Process Innovator.

▶ *Type 5:* Customers who need a specific, customized solution, often jointly developed with the supplier. In working with these customers, BASF acts as a Customized Solutions Provider.

▶ *Type 6:* Customers who want to reduce the cost and complexity of their operations by working with a supplier who will take over one or more of their processes. In working with these customers, BASF acts as a Value Chain Integrator.

As you can see, each of these six customer types has very different needs, ranging from the simplest to the most complex. BASF immediately recognized that no single customer service model would be appropriate for all six types of customers. The six types also did not map neatly or consistently against BASF's familiar organizational structure of product lines, itself an artifact of traditional inside-out thinking.

It was clear that BASF's methods of working with customers would have to be intelligently customized to fit specific customer segments as reflected in the six CIMs. This was the first big revelation delivered by the new Perspectives program. It led to a major new challenge: How could a huge, long-established corporation redesign its processes, structures, systems, and methods to better address the new and varied array of customer needs that BASF is called upon to meet?

BASF responded with another new process, named Pathfinder. In the Pathfinder system, a particular business unit within BASF assembles a cross-functional team to tackle a structured set of questions designed to generate a deeper understanding of specific customers—their own value chains, market requirements, industry trends, and more. The team meets with customer representatives to answer these questions and identify one or more CIMs that are most likely to meet the customer's emerging needs. Thus, interactions between customers and services teams were no longer dictated by one-size-fits-all processes that were uniform across a product line. Instead, they were tailored to the nature of the specific CIM being served, making BASF much more responsive to the *actual* needs and preferences of customers. This was a powerful process and organizational innovation that would prove to be as valuable to BASF and its customers as any product innovation might be.

Having designed the Pathfinder process, BASF's leadership realized the need to embed it—and the way of thinking it embodied—deep into the culture of the corporation. As an initial goal, leadership set a target of enabling 20 percent of BASF's marketing and sales professionals to be "effective change agents" by becoming masters of Pathfinder.

To launch this long-term culture-change program, BASF employees were engaged in the new approach to business through a series of workshops and learning activities. These included:

- Deep Dives into specific topics related to customer-centric innovation, such as value capturing and product launching
- Business Model Labs, which provided intensive coaching in skills like understanding customers

▸ Cross-Divisional Impact Groups, which helped BASF employees learn from one another as they work together on challenges such as implementing a specific CIM, improving the management of a particular brand, or launching a new product

▸ Impact Events, staged across Europe, Asia, and the Americas, designed to educate BASF team members about the new, collaborative approach to value creation

Note that one or more members of the corporation's board of directors participated in every Impact Event, sending a clear signal that this project was a high priority for the entire enterprise.

As Perspectives gained momentum, additional programs were created to ensure that awareness and understanding of the new system for innovation would continue to spread. For example, the Perspectives team designed Perspectives Key Concepts (PKC) workshops that all new professional hires were required to attend. Within the first year, more than 7,000 BASF employees had participated in PKC workshops. They became ambassadors for Perspectives and for its new way of interacting with customers, spreading the ideas and methods to others in their departments and functional areas. Business Forums bringing together scores of marketing, sales, and product managers from specific regions began to be held annually, providing venues in which best practices could be shared, discussed, and improved.

"We Help Our Customers to Be More Successful"

BASF's corporatewide effort to retool itself for an increasingly competitive, fast-changing business marketplace was summarized in an official corporate strategy statement. This statement was built around four crucial pillars, designed to summarize the basic elements of BASF's approach to business:

- ▶ *We earn a premium on our cost of capital*—expressing an emphasis on profitability, which BASF recognizes as a fundamental requirement for long-term survival and success.
- ▶ *We form the best team in the industry*—acknowledging the essential role of human talent in making business success possible.
- ▶ *We ensure sustainable development*—emphasizing the necessity for social engagement and environmental responsibility.
- ▶ *We help our customers to be more successful*—capturing the specific orientation of BASF as a business-to-business partner.

Of these four pillars, the fourth was the one that posed the biggest challenges for BASF, because it demanded a new level of customer intimacy, engagement, and "outside-in" orientation. The Perspectives program evolved as BASF's way of making this philosophical commitment into a practical, everyday reality.

Supported strongly by the BASF board, Jaffé and his team did a good job of mobilizing the organization's resources behind the spread of Perspectives into every corner of the business. As Jaffé observed just a few years after its launch, "Today, no one is asking 'What is Perspectives?' anymore." The power of Perspectives, now activated throughout BASF, has been reflected in sharply increased customer satisfaction measures, enhanced profitability, and a greatly improved reputation for BASF as an innovator among the world's great chemical companies.

One of the big changes in BASF's operating methods has been the increased emphasis on cocreation with customers. In the "old BASF," the company's brilliant chemists would work in their labs on developing and testing new molecules that they believed had the potential to serve useful roles in the real world. When the scientists were convinced they'd developed a product with valuable applications, they'd begin to work with the marketing, sales, and customer service teams to create a plan for bringing the innovation to market. Sometimes it worked, but sometimes it didn't; not every product developed in this way offered the ideal combination of performance attributes, price, and other characteristics that customers needed or wanted. Like companies in almost every business, BASF ended up with a mix of hit products and failures.

The new "outside-in" orientation fostered by the Perspectives team has changed the equation. Now BASF scientists increasingly work in partnership with their colleagues from the marketing, sales, and customer service functions as well as with multidisciplinary teams from BASF's customer firms. Rather than starting their experimentation with new molecules they hope will have some practical value, they start with the expressed needs of customers and then collaborate with those customers at every step of the process to ensure that every experiment, test, and redesign is focused on producing a product with powerful market appeal.

Finding Value in Unexpected Places: Tales of BASF Breakthroughs

BASF's thousands of scientists continue to produce a steady stream of scientific discoveries, just as they have for generations. What's changed is that today they are doing a better job of working with customers to cocreate products that generate value for both parties.

That's the story behind Boost, a new form of polyurethane originally discovered by BASF chemists and then developed by them in collaboration with Adidas into a groundbreaking foam for use in the soles of high-performance running shoes—a market into which BASF had previously never ventured.

So-called thermoplastic polyurethane (TPU for short) was a familiar BASF product long used in a variety of applications, such as electrical cables. But one day Frank Prissok, a chemist in a

BASF lab in Lemförde, Germany, noticed that by applying pressure and heat the material could be expanded into a foam, filled with tiny air pockets—"like popping corn in the microwave," as one of his colleagues explains. It was an interesting discovery—but what value could it have? The scientist had no idea.

Fortunately, he didn't shrug his shoulders and leave it at that. Instead, he decided to solicit input from his colleagues across the corporation. He filmed a number of short videos showing the characteristics of this new foam, now dubbed E-TPU, and circulated the videos among BASF professionals. One of these caught the attention of Martin Vallo, a marketing professional who'd been working with materials for shoe soles (already a significant market for BASF, though separate from the market for running shoes). He reached out to product experts at some of the leading running shoe makers.

The Adidas team members, who already knew Vallo well from their work together on other projects, were the most enthusiastic about the potential of the new foam. They were impressed by its unique qualities—high long-term durability, extreme flexibility, effectiveness under a wide range of temperature conditions, and, above all, outstanding resilience. E-TPU had the potential to give competitive runners an energy-fueling rebound effect that would boost their performance with every stride.

Adidas agreed to collaborate with BASF on perfecting E-TPU, and the cocreation process kicked into high gear. Vallo describes how it worked:

> You have to picture a whole bunch of techies engaged in discussions that were hard fought but always on an equal footing. Adidas had very clear ideas on what an insole from a new material should be able to perform, for instance, in terms of elasticity or temperature resistance. There were fundamental issues to be resolved too, such as whether a whole new set of tools or machinery would be needed . . . The

product was sent back to the lab on a regular basis to see whether certain properties could be improved even more by tweaking certain parameters. . . .

Just because something works in the lab doesn't mean that it's going to work on a large scale. . . . It's not easy to find the ideal process. A lot of fine-tuning is required. For that reason, we brought together BASF experts with different skills: chemists, plastics experts, engineers, project technicians.

Under an exclusive arrangement with BASF, Adidas brought E-TPU to market with the brand name of Boost in 2013. It caused an immediate sensation in the world of competitive running. Within a year, a new world record of 2:02:57 for the marathon was set by Kenyan Dennis Kimetto using a pair of Adidas shoes fitted with Boost soles. Other shoe companies that had turned down BASF's initial inquiries about the material even sued for the right to produce Boost-soled shoes of their own.

Years later, with new running sole materials from a range of companies having hit the market, Adidas is continuing to sell huge numbers of running shoes incorporating newly evolved versions of Boost, including the latest innovations, Ultraboost 19 and Pulseboot HD, both introduced in 2019. Boost is a tribute to the kind of long-term success that can be created through cocreative partnerships between a highly innovative company and a customer with an intimate knowledge of the needs and desires of the market.

Another vivid illustration of the degree to which the new culture of innovation has permeated BASF is the story of an unlikely product: Basotect foam, a sponge-like melamine resin that has become one of the company's greatest success stories.

For years, BASF sold Basotect as a soundproofing and insulating material for use in the construction and automotive industries. But one day, by sheer accident, a new quality of Basotect was discovered. During a sales call at a Japanese construction company, a BASF representative spilled a cup of coffee on a blueprint that had been spread out on the table. Hastily trying to mop up the spill, he grabbed the nearest material, which happened to be a slab of Basotect foam. When he applied the Basotect to the wet blueprint, not only was the spill absorbed but so was the ink. Wherever the Basotect touched, the blueprint became totally blank!

After the BASF sales rep apologized, he thought about what he had discovered. He shared his experience with the chemists at the office, and they realized that Basotect, when combined with water, becomes a powerful dye- and stain-remover.

In the past, this discovery might well have been dismissed within BASF as a mere novelty. In an engineering-centered culture where brilliant scientists are focused on researching specific issues, seemingly irrelevant data points may tend to be ignored. Furthermore, like many large corporations with divisions that pursue widely disparate technological and market opportunities, BASF's operations tended to be heavily siloed, making it difficult for ideas or problems that surfaced in one part of the company to get picked up on the radar of a different part. If "business as usual" had prevailed, it would have been easy for an accidental discovery made by a sales rep in BASF's construction business to have died there, never reaching the attention of anyone with interest in a product with stain-removing potential.

But in a company newly attuned to the importance of systematic innovation, that didn't happen. Instead, BASF launched a search for customers who might be looking for a substance with the newly discovered capabilities of Basotect. Within two years, it established an R&D partnership with Procter & Gamble (P&G), which led to the development of a household cleaning tool made from Basotect foam. Under the brand name of Mr. Clean Magic Eraser, it was dubbed one of the Best Inventions of 2004 and rapidly became one of P&G's fastest-growing product lines. By 2012, it had spawned a series of spin-off products, including the Magic Eraser Extra Power,

Magic Eraser Bath Scrubber, and Magic Eraser Select-a-Size, and surpassed its billionth unit sale. As of 2020, the Magic Eraser family of products is still going strong, a pillar of P&G's global profitability.

Incidentally, BASF has not neglected the other properties of Basotect foam. The company continues to market the product as a construction material with remarkable insulating and soundproofing qualities. In 2017, artist Doug Wheeler used 400 pyramids and 600 wedges of Basotect foam to construct a room at New York's Solomon R. Guggenheim Museum. The immersive experience creates an environment of near-perfect silence, relieved only by the faint recorded sounds of desert winds playing quietly over hidden speakers, all just a few feet away from the bustling traffic of Fifth Avenue. Titled *PSAD Synthetic Desert III*, the art installation was designed to induce the kind of "serene and silent escape" that only the "semi-anechoic chamber" made possible by BASF's chemical talents could provide.[4] Talk about the art of innovation!

Beyond the Product:
Business Model Innovation

Product innovations like Boost and Basotect foam will always play a big role in keeping BASF at the forefront of its industry. But the company's new focus on an outside-in orientation and cocreation with customers has also enabled innovation that goes beyond a stream of new products. BASF has become one of the world's masters of *business model innovation*—finding ways to rethink and redesign the entire array of relationships, processes, and systems that produces economic value for BASF, its customers, and all its stakeholders.

The work on developing the six CIMs that the Perspectives team led was a crucial starting point for BASF's evolution into a great business model innovator. Studying the CIMs helped

BASF's people understand the complexities involved in serving customers with widely differing needs and preferences. They came to recognize that developing a high-quality product was just the start of their innovative work. Equally important was mapping an entire chain of activities that would add crucial value for customers and other stakeholders in specific, highly targeted ways. This business model would define exactly how BASF would profit in a particular market—which meant that there was no one-size-fits-all model that would work in every market. In fact, choosing and refining the business model for a specific business is a highly complex, demanding innovative task that calls for teamwork, deep customer insight, flexibility, and creative thinking.

Once BASF made business model innovation into one of its core competencies, the company's leaders soon discovered just how complex such innovation can be. The new head of the Perspectives program, Dr. Uwe Hartwig, senior vice president, played a central role in driving this work.

Working with business analysts from the Institute of Technology Management at the University of St. Gallen in Switzerland, BASF's innovation experts actually created a set of printed cards depicting each of the possible business models they believed were theoretically applicable to various kinds of businesses. For example, one model is defined as the "Product and Effect Package" model, in which "a company not only produces a product, but also provides and sells value claims associated with it . . . The improved value proposition to the end consumer therefore enhances the willingness to pay for the complete package comprising product and associated claims. Depending on the industry, central tasks in this business model may include scientific testing and validation of claims, and/or interaction with regulatory bodies."

Another model is "Lock-In," in which "customers are locked into a vendor's world of products and services . . . This lock-in is either generated by technological mechanisms or substantial interdependencies of products or services." And a third is "Integrator," in which a company "is in command of the bulk of steps in a value-adding process. The control of all resources and capabilities in terms of value creation lies with the company."[5]

Using the models defined on these cards as touchpoints, the BASF Perspectives team set about analyzing the range of existing business models already being practiced within the corporation. Over the decades, teams dedicated to product development, marketing, and sales within various divisions and departments of BASF had semi-deliberately adapted a range of business models based on the challenges and opportunities they discovered around them.

When these various models were defined and codified by BASF's strategic analysts, they found that as many as 30 different models were in use around the organization out of some 45 possible models they'd defined. This is a remarkable number. In fact, BASF's innovation specialists believe that their company may actively operate using more different business models than any other corporation in the world.

Defining this range of business models was just the first step. The next step, which is happening in BASF operations around the world, is studying whether the current models are optimizing value creation for BASF and its customers. This is a task that requires a lot of creative what-if thinking. It may lead to the conclusion that the business model being used in a particular market needs to change—a challenging innovative process.

Sometimes, BASF operating divisions find themselves under positive pressure to change their business models. One starting point for a business model change may be a division finding that their sales and profitability are in long-term decline. In this case, without a change in business model, the entire division may be facing ultimate demise.

In other cases, one or more customers may ask the company to consider altering its way of doing business—by providing new services, for example, or by shifting the organizational boundaries that determine which company in a business partnership does what. In this sort of case, the new business model may be shaped through a cocreation process between customer and supplier.

Thus, as explained by Michael-Georg Schmidt, director of innovation excellence for BASF, the company has found that its CIM model is not just a list of six buckets into which each batch of customers can be sorted: "We need to constantly closely monitor the dynamics in the system because our customers' needs are always changing, which means our relationships with them need to change as well."

Business model innovation is no simple matter. Hartwig once estimated that it takes an average of 8 to 10 years to change a long-established business model. It usually happens in stages, with new activities being gradually introduced and old ones altered or eliminated, all involving close collaboration between BASF employees and customer teams.

Consider, for example, the way BASF's business model for providing paints and other coating materials to auto manufacturers has evolved over the years. At one time, BASF simply manufactured paints and sold these to the carmakers as finished products. This wasn't a very lucrative business for BASF; the division was constantly subject to price pressure from competing companies that might offer similar (though not necessarily equally good) paints at slightly lower prices. And the results that the automakers enjoyed weren't optimal; their factory teams didn't necessarily have the expertise needed to accurately define the best types of coatings or to apply them with minimal waste and the highest possible quality.

Beginning with Mercedes-Benz, BASF started working with its automaking customers to develop a more satisfactory business model. BASF experts began to be stationed at auto factories to serve as consultants and advisors on the painting process. Auto design and manufacturing teams started working closely with BASF chemists to develop paint and coating products more finely attuned to carmakers' needs. The boundaries between organizations and processes broke down as innovation morphed into cocreation.

Today, BASF offers what it calls its Integrated Process for Automotive Paint Procedures. Workers from BASF's coatings division take responsibility for finishing cars directly at the customer's factory. BASF manager John Fatura explains, "We like to work with our OEM [original equipment manufacturer] partners to determine what sustainable, automotive paint processes will work best in both their current and new facilities while meeting the demands they have in terms of operational costs and environmental standards." The savings generated by the resulting efficiencies go to reduce costs for the carmakers while also increasing the profits enjoyed by BASF—a true win-win.

BASF has gone on to apply business model innovation to an array of other businesses, in fields ranging from construction and mining to personal care products. Business model innovation isn't as widely known or understood as traditional product innovation. But as BASF has found, it can be even more powerful as a tool for business growth.

In my work as a corporate consultant, coach, and trainer, I've found that more and more companies today are focusing on business model innovation as a vital element of competitive adaptation. In a world where technological, social, cultural, and demographic changes are constantly shaking up marketplaces and creating both new opportunities and new competitive threats, companies can't assume that the familiar ways of doing business they've practiced for years will continue to work in the future. As you work on energizing your organization's innovating engine, make sure your team members are continually examining the ways your current business models are serving the needs of customers—or failing to do so. You may well discover—as BASF did—that responding to those evolving needs requires not just the creation of innovative products and services but also the design of entirely new ways of relating to your customers.

"Endless Opportunities"— the BASF Story of Innovation

In 2017, the Perspectives program at BASF came to an end. The task it had undertaken to jump-start a new way of innovating throughout BASF had been successfully accomplished. Out of some 15,000 eligible managers at the company, 12,000 had received training in the Perspectives approach to innovating, and 90 percent of BASF's product departments had worked through the Pathfinder process to improve their understanding of customer needs.

Today, the legacy of Perspectives is being carried on through a number of continuing innovation programs. New BASF employees are trained in the key concepts underlying Perspectives as part of a Marketing Starter Kit of tools, skills, and practices. And a separate department known as the Marketing and Sales Academy works to maintain company knowledge of innovating techniques and to train BASF employees and managers in how to use them. Through programs like these, innovating the Perspectives way has become a basic component of the corporation's DNA.

BASF's Schmidt is an eloquent advocate for the company's culture of innovation. He describes with special vividness the wide range of creative possibilities the company enjoys, as well as the innovative challenges these diverse options create:

> I think what is very exciting in the chemical industry is that you have touchpoints to all kinds of value chains and areas of human life, because chemistry is everywhere—in a kitchen table, in a smartphone, in a pencil, in the cosmetics in your purse. This means we have almost endless opportunities to innovate. The big question is figuring out which opportunities are most promising and which ones we want to focus on. This kind of focusing is the most important challenge for us.

As of 2021, BASF is focusing its innovating model on challenges in a number of specific areas, including the development of digital and service-based business models, and the design and implementation of processes that enhance the environmental sustainability of BASF and its customers. The goal is to prepare BASF to be part of the emerging circular economy that experts say will be needed to support a world in which growing populations put increasing pressure on limited resources.

BASF's approach to innovation illustrates some of the crucial insights that leaders of all kinds of companies can use to enhance their own organizations' innovative capabilities. Once you take *innovating by anyone, anytime, anywhere* as your goal, you can begin turning your organization into a true innovating engine.

KEY TAKEAWAYS FROM CHAPTER 1

- Every organization, no matter how successful, needs to develop an approach to innovating that is *systematic* rather than haphazard.
- Innovating must be *embedded* in every part of an organization rather than relegated to an R&D department or other specialized unit.
- An *innovating team* armed with proven tools and techniques can play a crucial role in spreading the methods and culture of innovating throughout the organization.
- An organization's corporate culture must be shaped to be open to innovative approaches, such as *cocreation* with customers.
- Innovating involves much more than just product development (important as that is). More complex forms of innovating, such as *business model innovation*, can be even more powerful ways to create more value both for customers and for the companies that serve them.

2

EXECUTION AND INNOVATING

TWIN ENGINES POWERED BY EVERYONE IN THE ORGANIZATION

The materials company W. L. Gore was founded in 1958 by maverick engineer Wilbert Gore and his wife, Genevieve, usually known as Bill and Vieve. Bill Gore was fascinated by the innovative potential of a then little-known substance known as polytetrafluoroethylene (PTFE). A few years later, PTFE would become famous as a coating for cookware under the brand name of Teflon. But in the meantime, Bill Gore and his son Bob had discovered that PTFE could be "stretched" in the lab to form a microporous structure that is 70 percent air.

The Gores commercialized PTFE as Gore-Tex, a waterproof yet breathable fabric membrane ideal for creating all-weather garments. To this day, it's considered the gold standard for outdoor wear. And dozens of other uses have been found for Gore-Tex, from making meshes, sutures, and other medical appliances to serving as a laminate to help preserve fragile illuminated manuscripts from the Middle Ages.

In the decades since then, the Gore company has grown by discovering creative new uses for materials—not just Gore-Tex, but a continually expanding range of other materials created using modern chemical methods. This track record of successful innovation has its roots in principles and practices that go back to founders Bill and Vieve Gore and that continue to shape the organization today.

One of the practices pioneered under Bill Gore's leadership was that of encouraging all of the company's associates (as they are always called) to spend 10 percent of their time "dabbling" in projects that appealed to them. Over time, Gore's Dabble Time system produced some of the biggest business successes enjoyed by the enterprise (again, the term that Gore prefers).

Some of the most famous innovative breakthroughs in Gore's illustrious history had their origin in Dabble Time projects launched by individual associates. For example, back in the early 1990s, engineer Dave Myers, an associate in Gore's medical division and an avid biker, noticed that a PTFE coating made the cables on his mountain bike especially resistant to oil and grit. Curiosity piqued, he wondered whether the same concept might protect and enhance the sound of guitar strings. That led to three years of tests and experimentation by Myers and a few like-minded colleagues whose support and help he solicited. Ultimately, the team developed guitar strings that hold their tone three times longer than the then-current standard. Today, Gore's ELIXIR brand guitar strings are the industry's bestsellers.

Two Engines, Two Different Modes of Operation

The story of how Myers's Dabble Time investigations led to a whole new business opportunity for W. L. Gore illustrates the first requirement for enhancing your organization's innovation capabilities. Every organization needs to operate two different engines simultaneously: an *execution engine* and an *innovating engine.*

The execution engine is about doing your current work as skillfully, efficiently, and flawlessly as possible. The execution engine drives how products get made, services get delivered, records get maintained, sales get transacted, and other daily activities get completed. The innovating engine, on the other hand, may seem to get *nothing* done. It's about looking for new ideas—imagining new products or services, designing new work methods or processes, experimenting with new technologies, learning about new markets, or investigating customer (and noncustomer) needs and desires that you've never previously tried to address.

Many organizations understand the need for both an execution engine and an innovating engine. But many make the mistake of thinking that the two engines ought to be separately staffed, organized, and managed. Some assume that a traditional team of scientists or engineers staffing a research and development (R&D) department can be expected to churn out all the innovations that the organization needs. The fact is that *all* of your company's employees should find themselves working in *both* engines, dedicating some of their time and energy to execution and some of both to innovating. But they'll need to adopt dramatically differing mindsets depending on which engine they are part of at a given moment.

Note that this is an alternative approach to building what is often called an "ambidextrous organization," capable of looking to the future while simultaneously perfecting the way it operates in the present day.[1] The traditional concept of the ambidextrous organization assumes that different teams focus on these two contrasting tasks. However, I recommend that "ambidexterity" should be embedded in every organizational department and level, beginning with each individual employee.

The mindset of the execution engine is skeptical, logical, demanding, and rigorous. In organizing and managing the execution engine, efficiency is the paramount goal. Thus, in defining what tasks will be performed by the execution engine and exactly how those tasks will be handled, all the many financial metrics used to define business success—return on investment (ROI), return on equity (ROE), earnings before interest and taxes (EBIT), the Berry ratio, and more—may be brought into play. Everything the execution engine does must be justified as a contribution to value, either for the customers or for the organization; anything that fails to pass this test must be ruthlessly improved, streamlined, or eliminated.

Managing the innovating engine is quite a different matter. The mindset of the innovating engine is open-minded, imaginative, accepting, and flexible. Ideas and possibilities that are floated by the innovating engine are—at least temporarily— embraced without concern about whether they are practical, how to make them happen, how they will be used to generate revenues, and what sort of profit margins they might yield. If the ideas excite a strong enough response from members of the organization, there will be plenty of time later to evaluate and test them according to logical principles and cost-benefit analyses before they are implemented by the execution engine.

Table 2.1 shows some of the systematic differences between the execution engine and the innovating engine. You'll find that some of the contrasts highlighted in this table will become clearer as you make your way through the chapters in this book.

Both the execution engine and the innovating engine are essential to the long-term success of the organization. But in many organizations, the innovating engine doesn't get the attention it deserves. That's understandable. After all, the execution engine is what keeps the organization running on a day-to-day basis. If it shuts down or stops working efficiently, the customers disappear, the revenues and profits dry up, and the business quickly dies.

By contrast, the value created by the innovating engine isn't as obvious, and it takes longer to come to fruition. In the short run, an organization can get by without innovating, just by doing

TABLE 2.1   The Execution Engine Versus the Innovating Engine

	Execution Engine	Innovating Engine
STRATEGIC ORIENTATION		
Strategic Objective	Competing successfully	Disrupting the industry
Organizational Perspective	Supplier-side view—focused on outperforming the competition, being best in the industry, offering good value to existing customers	Customer-side view—focused on discovering ways to create superior value for both customers and noncustomers, whether internal or external
STRUCTURAL ORIENTATION		
Main Objective	Executing current strategy	Exploring future strategy
Organizational Structure	Hierarchical, bureaucratic, multi-layered, top-down, siloed, formal, primary organization (CEO and C-suite, middle managers, and frontline employees)	Flat, networked, team-based, cross-departmental, and cross-layered, flexible, informal, parallel organization (I-Team with I-Committee, I-Coordinators, and I-Coaches)
Mental and Physical Space	Execution space (Reality Room)	Exploration or innovation space (Dream Room, innovation lab, garage)
PROCESS ORIENTATION		
Underlying Key Processes	Planning, budgeting, consolidating, reporting, marketing and sales, operational processes	Creation, integration, and reframing processes
Dominant Cognitive Process	Problem solving—a convergent process centered on finding the optimal solution to the problem at hand	Problem finding—a divergent process centered on looking for new problems to solve for customers and noncustomers
Dominant Control, Incentive, and Measurement Model	Outcome-based control, incentive, and measurement model	Behavior-based control, incentive, and measurement model
Typical Ways of Working	Careful periodic planning, tight controls	Trial and error, experimentation
	Failure avoidance	Embracing of fast failure and post-mortem learning
	Rigorous analysis	Rigorous testing
	Actions justified by business case	Actions undertaken in a spirit of exploration
	Arm's-length customer relationships	Deep customer immersion
	Periodic reviews	Continuous reviews
	Implementation, disciplined execution	Experimentation, exploration
	Optimization	Learning
	Maximization (comprehensive hypothesis testing)	Minimization (hypothesis building with fast experimentation, fast prototyping)
CULTURAL ORIENTATION		
Characteristic Attitudes and Behaviors	Focused, disciplined, and rigorous	Open-minded, flexible, and willing to expand thinking
	Culture of urgency and results	Empathetic and tolerant
	Linear, logical, and reason-based thinking	Trusting and listening to emotions and first impressions
	Rational checking and testing based on precise and tangible data	Patient and open to "crazy" or outside-the-box ideas

the same things it has always done. It takes time for the failure to innovate to take its toll on the organization; it happens only as changing markets, evolving customer needs, and emerging competitive threats gradually make the old ways of doing things obsolete. When the damage becomes too significant to ignore, company leaders finally realize—too late—that they should have been paying attention to the innovating engine all along.

The smartest business leaders don't let that happen. They understand that they need to create, legitimize, protect, and (most important) *systematize* the workings of their organization's innovating engine. If the company is going to survive and thrive in changing times, the innovating engine must be maintained and kept running, engaging the creative efforts of people throughout the organization, in every division and department and at all three operational levels: among frontline employees, midlevel managers, and senior leaders.

This poses a daunting yet fascinating challenge. It's one thing to say that every member of an organization should participate both in execution and in innovating; it's quite another to make it happen in reality. How is it possible to inculcate both the execution mindset and the innovating mindset in the same individual? How can an organization simultaneously run its innovating engine and its execution engine, with their highly contrasting cultures, in parallel and with the participation of the very same people?

Examining the unusual management practices of highly innovative companies like W. L. Gore can help us answer these questions.

Beyond Dabble Time: How W. L. Gore Embeds Innovating Throughout the Organization

We've already mentioned one of the secrets that W. L. Gore developed to trigger activity on the part of its innovating engine—the concept of Dabble Time, which encouraged associates to set aside 10 percent of their time as sacred to experimentation, with no promised or required payoff. Other highly innovative organizations have used similar systems to foster the creative energies of their employees. The 3M Corporation, for example, is famous for its 15 Percent Rule, which mandates that engineers and scientists may spend up to 15 percent of their time on "experimental doodling," playing with out-of-the-box ideas that may lead to unexpected opportunities. Breakthrough products ranging from Post-it Notes to the first electronic stethoscope equipped with Bluetooth technology have emerged as a result of the 15 Percent Rule.[2] Google, Hewlett-Packard, and software company Maddock Douglas are other examples of companies that have embraced the practice of explicitly giving employees free time simply to think, with no return on investment expected or required.

Creating and promulgating this kind of policy—and widely publicizing it, as these companies do—encourages employees to consciously switch from the execution mindset to the innovating mindset for part of every week, which is a powerful first step in ensuring that the innovating engine gets the idea-fuel it needs to run.

But Dabble Time is just one element that went into building W. L. Gore's high-performance innovating engine. More fundamental has been a series of core beliefs and guiding principles that are intended to define the company's way of treating people. The goal is to shape an environment in which innovation by everyone is encouraged and empowered. Those core beliefs are:

▸ Belief in the individual, which includes the potential of each associate to help the company grow and succeed
▸ Belief in the power of small teams, in which associates can make good decisions and produce quality work
▸ Belief that "we're all in the same boat," which means that associates have a vested interest in the success of the company and should make decisions accordingly

▶ Belief in the long-term view, which should guide every decision an associate makes

The guiding principles that associates are expected to follow in their work include *freedom, fairness, commitment,* and *waterline*—the last referring to the importance of avoiding decisions that might create holes "below the waterline," thereby potentially "sinking the ship," whose well-being all associates should protect. Taken together, these beliefs and principles, which guided W. L. Gore in the time of Bill and Vieve and still animate the organization today, play a key role in nurturing the company's innovating engine and encouraging all associates to play an active role in it.[3]

Another element of W. L. Gore's culture that helps it maintain an unusually robust innovating engine is its organizational structure. Gore strives to be relatively free of the hierarchical constraints that govern most companies and limit what employees are able to do, how they communicate with one another, and even how they are permitted to think. Instead, the company's so-called lattice structure encourages the formation of small teams, free-flowing communication, and leadership through coaching and influencing rather than commanding and controlling.

This philosophy of management can also be traced back to founder Bill Gore, who liked to say that "authoritarians cannot impose commitments, only commands." Because Gore wanted a company filled with people who were genuinely committed to their work, he insisted that associates should be permitted—nay, required—to negotiate their job assignments and responsibilities with their peers rather than having them imposed by a "boss."

It may take a while for new associates accustomed to traditional management methods to make sense of Gore's lattice structure. One Gore newcomer, unable to figure out what was expected of her, kept asking her colleagues, "Who's my boss?" Finally, someone told her, "Stop using the B-word." She eventually figured out that she was expected to define her own work and join a team of colleagues who were engaged in projects she found interesting and compelling. She ended up becoming a top performer, what Gore calls a "category champion."[4]

For this associate, it took a while to understand and accept the idea that she was supposed to innovate as well as execute. That's understandable, since the dual mindset required is not commonly understood or encouraged in most businesses . . . which helps to explain why so many businesses struggle to innovate.

Some management theorists refer to the nonhierarchical, self-guided management style that W. L. Gore pioneered as *open allocation.* A similar system has been adopted by a number of other companies, including the successful video game developer Valve, profiled later in this book. As you can imagine, it may be challenging to implement, especially as a company becomes bigger and more complicated. This helps to explain why W. L. Gore was called, in a 2019 profile in the *Financial Times,* "the company others try and fail to imitate."[5]

Against the odds, Gore has managed to preserve its unconventional management style even as it has grown and diversified. In the decades since Gore was founded in 1958, the enterprise has expanded into a multidivisional corporation with more than 10,000 employees and annual revenues of $3.7 billion (2019). To maintain the innovative flow in such a large, complex institution, Gore has developed a number of systems to help its associates focus their energies on projects with the potential to create real value both for customers and the enterprise, while still remaining free to choose their own organizational roles and manage their own time. These systems, in turn, have continued to evolve and morph in response to economic, technological, and environmental changes, while remaining fundamentally true to the core beliefs and guiding principles on which the company was built.

One of these systems is a way of developing innovative concepts into established business projects. In their earliest stages, the ideas generated by Gore associates are given a chance to germinate freely, without being subject to economic or other tests of viability. Eventually, ideas that appear to have business potential are tested, winnowed, and driven through an "innovation funnel" system that ensures the best ideas are brought to fruition. One part of this funnel is a three-stage review process called "Real, Win, Worth." A cross-functional team studies the concept and asks three key questions:

- ▶ *Real:* Does this idea represent a *real* business opportunity?
- ▶ *Win:* If we follow this idea into a new marketplace, do we have the potential to *win* in that space?
- ▶ *Worth:* Are the potential financial rewards *worth* investing the company's time, money, and other resources?

When the answers to all three questions are positive, the idea is passed on to a project team that is given the funding needed to research and develop it further. In this way, the Real, Win, Worth process serves as just one link in a chain of activities that connects the innovating engine and the execution engine. Ideas that pass the Real, Win, Worth test may grow into business units in their own right that are managed and run as profit-making contributors to the enterprise, just like the other parts of the W. L. Gore execution engine.

Gore's innovation funnel system differs from the conventional R&D process found in most companies. One difference, of course, is that everyone in the organization is a potential source of an innovative idea—not just a handful of innovation specialists in the R&D department. But perhaps the most significant difference is the open-ended nature of the idea germination stage, and the patience extended to Gore associates during it. As mentioned, Myers experimented with his idea for coating guitar strings with PTFE for three years, and even recruited help from other employees in the company, before seeking authorization to launch a formal business initiative around it. Only then did Myers's concept become subject to the usual corporate tests of marketability, profitability, and other performance indicators.

If you want your innovating engine to be as creative and productive as possible, you need to make sure it remains truly free from the limiting constraints that normal management expectations impose. Achieving this within a profit-driven business that is competing for survival and success in a demanding marketplace can be a tricky balancing act. So far, W. L. Gore has pulled it off, using an innovation system that is more egalitarian and unstructured than most organizational leaders would choose.

Today, Gore's innovative capabilities have led to an impressive array of product lines that extend far beyond the outdoor adventurer's gear for which the enterprise is best known. They range from the popular Glide brand of dental floss and textiles woven from a variety of PTFE fiber used in the protective gear worn by NASA astronauts to acoustic vents for smartphones and personal computers and medical stent grafts used in more than 40 million implant recipients around the world.

The vibrancy of Gore's innovating engine has helped to make it an unusually successful enterprise. It has also made it a magnet for talented and creative people from around the world. In fact, Gore has been one of just a handful of companies to appear on *Fortune* magazine's annual "Best Companies to Work For" list every year since the list was launched in 1998, earning the company a spot on the magazine's "Great Place to Work Legends" list in 2017.

Freeing people to innovate can be a great way to help your organization prevail in the ever-intensifying wars for talent.

The Value Test: Assessing the Value Created by an Innovative Idea

Gore's Real, Win, Worth process is part of the system by which the company selects innovative ideas for further development. Every organization with a healthy innovating engine needs such a system. One simple tool that you may want to integrate into your idea-generating system is what I like to call the Value Test. Based loosely on an approach described by business professors Adam Brandenburger and Harborne Stuart, the Value Test provides a mental discipline that managers can use to evaluate an innovating idea. All it requires is that you ask team members who are proposing an innovating idea a set of specific questions in a particular order. The answers to these questions will generate useful insights into the value that the idea may create.[6]

As illustrated in Figure 2.1, the Value Test treats your organization as a supplier that acquires resources from its own suppliers; transforms them into a product, service, or process; and then offers or sells it to a customer. In this process of exchange, the customer has a problem or desire that the supplier claims to solve or match, for which the customer is willing to pay a certain amount. *Willingness to pay* (WTP) is defined as the maximum amount the customer is prepared to exchange to receive the offered good; *price* (P) is defined as the actual price the supplier charges for the good; and *cost* (C) is defined as the amount of money, sacrifice, or effort that goes into producing the good.

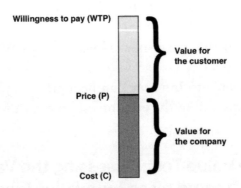

FIGURE 2.1 The Value Test

The interplay among these three elements defines the value created for the customer and for the company. *Value for the customer* is defined by the expression WTP – P. That is, the customer's willingness to pay for the company's product minus the price represents customer surplus, the amount of value captured and perceived by the customer side. When working with students or clients, I refer to this in several ways—as customer value, customer delight, or even customer happiness.

Meanwhile, value for the company is defined by the expression P – C. The price received from the customer minus the total cost of producing the product or service represents the amount of value captured by the firm.

As you might imagine, measuring the customer willingness to pay (WTP) and the supplier cost (C) is important to the execution engine when it needs to design a pricing strategy for a new product or service. However, when we're working in innovating mode, we don't necessarily need to precisely assess these elements. The benefit of the Value Test framework lies in its value as a mental structure that can guide your thinking and suggest the questions to ask when testing whether an innovating idea is worth further exploration.

The first question to ask is, *Will this idea increase the customer's willingness to pay for the product or service?* The second question is, *Will this idea lead to lower cost for the company in producing the product or service (for example, through greater efficiency)?* The answers to these questions will help you answer the overarching question: *Is this a good idea that deserves further exploration?*

Notice that it's not necessary to use the illustration shown in Figure 2.1 or even the name "Value Test" when performing this exercise with your team members (though there's certainly no harm in doing so). Simply asking these questions consistently whenever an innovating idea is presented will have an impact on the way your team members think. Soon they will be asking themselves the same questions almost automatically, thus training themselves to become more highly skilled evaluators of an innovating idea's potential.

The Process Is the Hero:
The Innovating Engine at Samsung

Freeing individual team members to tinker with their own ideas through a practice like W. L. Gore's Dabble Time isn't the only way of jump-starting your company's innovating engine. Some highly innovative organizations have employed other practices that are more formal and disciplined while still making room for the open-ended spirit that makes creativity possible. One example is the Korean electronics giant Samsung.

Founded in 1938 as a multibusiness trading company, Samsung entered the electronics industry in the late 1960s. For the next two decades, Samsung was best known as a competent maker of "me-too" products that emulated the designs and features of such well-known innovators as Sony and Panasonic. During the 1970s and 1980s, Samsung developed manufacturing efficiencies and marketing methods that allowed it to compete on price and gradually claim a small but steadily growing share of the consumer electronics marketplace.

Samsung's leaders understood that, in the long run, manufacturing excellence alone would not allow them to rival Microsoft, IBM, or Apple on the global business stage. But their early efforts at innovation often fell flat. Samsung came out with one of the world's first MP3 music players in 1999. Yet two years later, Apple introduced its iPod, coupling it with iTunes software and a website where a vast trove of music was instantly available for purchase. The innovative combination swept away the competition, including Samsung. The company's then-CEO, Yun Jong Yong, was quoted as saying that Samsung had become "a good company," but added, "we still have a lot of things to do before we're a great company."[7]

In the years since then, things have changed. Samsung has gradually risen to world leadership as an innovator in screen technology, chip design, smartphone software and hardware, tablet computing, and other categories. Since 2009, the company's line of Galaxy smartphones has been a leader in innovation, offering breakthroughs in the immersive screen experience, intuitive input tools like the S Pen stylus, leading-edge security tools like biometric authentication, and advances in wireless charging technology.

Samsung's talent for innovating has not gone unnoticed. In 2019, the company was ranked fourth in the world in the annual Most Innovative Tech Brands study conducted by the New York–based Brand Keys consultancy, its sixth straight year in the top five. In the same year, it was ranked fifth in the list of global innovation companies as chosen by Boston Consulting Group.

Even one-time skeptics have been won over by Samsung's newfound creativity. In late 2019, technology journalist Jeremy Horwitz, a self-proclaimed long-time Apple aficionado, after attending product presentations by both Apple and Samsung, reluctantly wrote, "I must concede that the companies' respective events have firmly established Samsung as the consumer electronics innovator to watch in 2020."[8]

Samsung has reached this level of innovative excellence through the painstaking, decades-long process of building an innovating engine that focuses on intensively training team members in methods for problem solving, imagining new technologies, and then converting these technological ideas into practical products with broad market appeal. Samsung believes that having a clearly defined *process* for innovation is more important than encouraging employees to dabble creatively on their own, and they've used this approach to forge an impressive track record of innovation.

One key to Samsung's emergence as an electronics innovator was the company's adoption of TRIZ, a system for problem solving originally developed back in the 1940s by—of all people—a Russian inventor and science-fiction author named Genrich Altshuller. The TRIZ system encourages would-be innovators to analyze the contradictions and failures inherent in current technologies, and then to use these findings as stepping-stones toward imagining new and better solutions. After experimenting with TRIZ for a year, Samsung reported generating 50 new patents as a result. Excited by what they saw happening, in 2003 company leaders set about training thousands of employees in the methodology, using a textbook by Samsung executive Hyo June Kim that translated the concepts of TRIZ into Korean.[9] "The use of TRIZ can change the uncreative to the creative," declared SeHo Cheong, managing director of Samsung Mobile Display division and a dedicated acolyte of TRIZ.[10]

As I'll discuss later in this book, a number of methodologies for innovation have been developed through the years. TRIZ is one of these. These methodologies offer varying ways of examining business challenges, asking probing questions about existing products and processes, analyzing the marketplace, understanding customer needs and preferences, and so on. The systems share many common attributes, but each one has its distinctive features, which means your organization may find itself drawn to one methodology rather than another.

Many experts on innovating have strong preferences for one or another of these methodologies. I personally like the Blue Ocean approach made famous through a classic 2005 book by Professor W. Chan Kim and Professor Renée Mauborgne. Through the years, I've taught the Blue Ocean tools to many corporate clients, who have used the tools with great success to drive their own innovating engines.

However, I take a somewhat contrarian position when it comes to innovating methodologies—namely, I am basically agnostic when it comes to choosing one system over another. My experience and observations suggest that no methodology has a monopoly on innovative techniques or good results; many different tool sets and practices can be helpful when it comes to generating, testing, and implementing innovative ideas. In fact, I think it can often be helpful to organizations to experiment with various innovating methodologies and even to deliberately shift from one system to another from time to time. When you make use of varying methodologies as your needs and objectives evolve, the innovating habits of your people can be repeatedly refreshed with new ways of thinking, often leading to a fresh burst of creativity.

Samsung itself illustrates the way two or more methodologies can be used effectively by a single company. Although Samsung is closely associated with the use of TRIZ, the company's entire innovation program was largely influenced by Chan Kim and Renée Mauborgne, the creators of Blue Ocean Strategy, and processes suggested by Kim and Mauborgne were among those that helped jump-start Samsung's innovating engine.[11]

Strictly speaking, it's probably a bit simplistic to say that any single methodology "can change the uncreative to the creative," in Cheong's words. But a well-designed innovation methodology can help unlock the innate creativity most people have inside them. TRIZ and Blue Ocean Strategy appear to have done this for Samsung.

In my view, the value of the TRIZ methodology for Samsung is based not so much on any specific attributes of that methodology, but rather in the company's adoption and dissemination of a *systematic process* for innovating. The simple fact that the company considered the mission of innovation urgent enough to ask thousands of its employees to spend days studying the process and applying it to their current challenges provided a powerful jolt of energy to Samsung's innovating engine. It sent a clear message to everyone at Samsung: *Executing your current job is important. But equally important is innovating our future. Let's work on doing this together!*

Another step in Samsung's rise to the top of the innovation heap was the establishment of the firm's Value Innovation Program (VIP) Center. Located near Samsung's factory complex 20 miles south of Seoul, this facility was originally opened in 1998 with a core focus on process streamlining and quality improvement. But in 2004, its purpose was reimagined and its emphasis on fundamental innovation was intensified. Now it is a place where engineers, programmers, designers, and marketing managers gather to imagine entirely new product ideas and develop plans for transforming them into realities.

Open 24 hours a day, the VIP Center is equipped with project rooms, sleeping quarters, a kitchen, recreational facilities, and even a traditional Japanese-style bath. Crucially, the individuals assigned to project teams at the center are *not* a separate corps of R&D specialists. Instead, they are ordinary Samsung employees with various skill sets, backgrounds, and operational functions—people who spend most of their time running the company's execution engine. Periodically, however, they are asked to shed that everyday job and instead become components of the innovating engine, tackling a particularly thorny challenge that deserves their undivided attention.

Employees live at the center for weeks at a time, guided by a team of "value innovation specialists" who facilitate their deliberations. These employees analyze customer survey data, study products from rival manufacturers, and brainstorm ways to leapfrog the competition. They spend time designing and redesigning potential new products, adding, modifying, and shedding features in search of the sweet spot where the perfect market-maximizing innovation is waiting. It's fascinating, sometimes grueling, work, and it involves a serious commitment of time, energy, and resources. In fact, the leaders of the company divisions from which the participants are drawn are asked to sign a pledge agreeing to let them remain at the center, away from their regular jobs, until the innovative project has been successfully completed.[12]

Samsung has found that concentrating this much brainpower on concocting new ideas can generate amazing levels of innovation. It happens not because any one or a few of the engineers, scientists, designers, or executives working at the VIP Center are particularly brilliant or gifted. The crucial factor is the organized, focused dedication of a diverse group of people engaged in a systematic process of innovating. The result is an innovating engine that generates new ideas and then repeatedly improves and refines them. In a very real sense, the process itself is the hero.

To enhance and expand this impressive innovating capability, Samsung has gone on to open additional innovation hubs in locations around the world, including a $1 billion center in San Jose in California's Silicon Valley and smaller sites in Menlo Park (adjacent to Stanford University), New York City, Tel Aviv, and Paris.

Today, the spirit of innovating has spread beyond the arena of product design to impact other departments of Samsung. For example, under the leadership of guru Emmanuel Malard, Samsung has become one of the world's most innovative marketing organizations. Since becoming Samsung's consumer and market insight manager in 2010, Malard has built a research division that conducts more than 150 market studies per year, giving the company a unique depth of insight into the evolving interests, preferences, and needs of consumers. When a customer buys a Samsung smartphone, he or she may be targeted for an interview after 30 days and then at varying intervals thereafter, allowing Samsung's analysts to track how the customer's experience with the product may be changing. And when the company wants to experiment with new marketing techniques, it uses innovative methods to measure and analyze the results in real time. For example, when the European-based marketing team decided to try using a billboard displaying Korean-language messages on the Place de la Concorde in Paris, some managers in Korea were skeptical. Malard's research division deployed a team of analysts equipped with tablets to measure consumer reactions on the spot, providing concrete data that allowed the billboard messages to be adjusted and enhanced within hours.[13]

It seems clear that the innovating engine that Samsung's leadership decided to begin building in the late 1990s is going strong, generating creative activities involving participants from throughout the organization.

None of this is to say that Samsung's quest to improve its innovating capacity is finished. Outside observers say that Samsung is still more skilled as a process engineering innovator than a product innovator. In other words, their special talent lies in making existing products faster, better, and cheaper, rather than in imagining entirely new product concepts and turning them into reality.[14] Others say that the company's innovating engine, while effective, may not be sustainable: some employees feel that the VIP Center, where tough innovating goals and challenging deadlines are set and enforced, applies excessive force rather than a spirit of freewheeling experimentation to the process of creative thinking. Perhaps in part for this reason, Samsung reportedly suffers from higher rates of attrition among its young recruits than it would like.

Signs suggest that Samsung is working to remedy these potential problems. As of early 2021, the company features an unusual three-person CEO office, manned by executives who are all relatively youthful, both chronologically and in their business outlook. Samsung has also expanded its level of international R&D with partners in North America and India, and it is intensifying its efforts to import talent from outside the company.

In these and other ways, it appears that Samsung is seeking to redesign an already formidable innovating engine to make it even more powerful for the challenges ahead—good news for the company's shareholders, not so good for its competitors.

Innovating Engines Take Many Forms and May Evolve Over Time

Your organization may choose to create a physical home for your innovating engine, the way Samsung did when it launched its VIP Center. The Walt Disney Company has long been admired as one of the world's most creative organizations. Its well-known system for innovation involves moving among three physical spaces—a Dream Room, a Criticism Room, and a Reality Room—to facilitate the shifts in thinking and focus required first to generate, then to test, and then to implement new ideas.[15] You too may find that dedicating a portion of your company offices, labs, or workshops to creativity is an effective way of signaling your commitment to innovating and inviting team members to participate in it.

On the other hand, rather than locating innovation in a specific physical place, you may prefer to encourage employees to set aside personal time and energy for innovation as companies like W. L. Gore do. In fact, the two approaches are not mutually exclusive. As I'll explain in the next chapter, Gore also operates its own innovation center, though with an approach and purpose different from those employed at Samsung's VIP Center. There's no reason employees can't incorporate freewheeling innovative thinking into their daily routines while also having the chance to periodically spend time working with colleagues at a dedicated facility where innovation is practiced 24/7.

In addition, many companies now locate their innovating engines, entirely or partially, in a virtual space accessible via the internet or an internal digital network. For example, Bayer, the global pharmacology and life sciences corporation based in Germany, operates a powerful innovating engine that includes a digital platform called WeSolve. Open to all Bayer employees, this online space allows anyone to post information about a problem they are wrestling with and invite input, ideas, and potential solutions from anyone else. At any given time, some 200 challenges, large and small, may be found on the WeSolve site, and Bayer people from around the world are participating in helping to address them.

In Chapter 9, I'll describe Bayer's innovating engine in more detail, and I'll explain how WeSolve came to be. But for the moment, notice how creating a virtual innovating space like WeSolve offers a number of advantages:

- ▶ A virtual innovating space is *inclusive*—anyone, anywhere with access to the company's intranet can contribute to the innovating process. On WeSolve, a problem posted by a technician in a lab in Germany may trigger helpful responses from a scientist in the United States, a marketing manager in Italy, a logistics expert in Japan, or an engineer in Brazil—and perhaps from all four.
- ▶ It's *continually active*—any Bayer employee with a few minutes to spare can log on to WeSolve, browse the currently featured challenges, and engage with any issue for which the employee may have something valuable to offer.
- ▶ It's *economical*—it allows professionals from around the organization and across the globe to interact with one another instantly, without the cost and inconvenience of convening a workshop or conference that requires time-consuming, expensive travel.
- ▶ It's *safe*—in a world where health challenges like the COVID-19 pandemic of 2020 can make face-to-face meetings complicated and risky, working together in a virtual space is worry-free.

Not every innovating activity can be conducted virtually. Sometimes there's no substitute for the intense personal engagement that happens when people spend time in one another's company for hours or even days or weeks, hashing out complicated challenges together. In-person activities like passing around product samples, assembling prototypes, drawing and redrawing sketches, and conducting real-time experiments may be difficult or impossible in a virtual space. So most organizations will want to supplement their online innovating programs with face-to-face gatherings when possible.

But whether your innovating space is physical, virtual, or a combination of both, you need to make your innovating engine sacred—that is, protected from the intrusion of the execution mindset—and available to everyone. Each employee must be encouraged and expected to regularly step away from the daily execution routine and engage in innovating activities. Innovating needs to be listed as a responsibility in each worker's job description and discussed as part of the conversation during the annual performance review.

Note, however, that I don't recommend penalizing frontline employees for a perceived failure to innovate during their performance review. Experience shows that innovative ideas can't be generated on command, and it would be wrong to punish people for not generating them. Instead, emphasize the positive side of the equation by encouraging frontline employees to innovate so they will feel free and empowered to do so.

The message you want to send to everyone in your organization is simple: It's important to do your current work and to do it well—but it's equally important to take part in imagining your organization's tomorrow and helping to bring it into being. The creative energy of every member of your team is needed to ensure that your innovating engine is running at full capacity.

KEY TAKEAWAYS FROM CHAPTER 2

- Every organization needs to develop two very different capabilities: the power to do its current work flawlessly (the *execution engine*) and the power to imagine brand-new products and processes (the *innovating engine*).
- Don't segregate your innovating engine into a separate business unit staffed only by R&D specialists. Every employee in every department needs to be able to work in *both engines*—and to adopt the mindset each engine demands.
- A range of methodologies can be used to inspire and guide the work of your innovating engine. The specific methodology you choose is less important than having a *systematic process* that encourages everyone to focus on innovating.
- Your innovating engine may or may not be located in a separate physical space—but it must be *accessible to everyone* who works for you.
- Encouraging everyone to take part in innovating can help make your company more attractive to the most creative, engaged, and energized people in the workforce.

3

THE INNOVATING PERSPECTIVE

THE SUPPLIER-SIDE VIEW VERSUS
THE CUSTOMER-SIDE VIEW

When it comes to innovation, big government doesn't have the greatest reputation. That applies to almost every US government agency you can think of, from the Post Office to the Department of Education. And it includes the biggest government operation in human history—the US military. The Pentagon spends almost $700 billion a year, and it has historically played a role in some incredibly important innovations, up to and including the development of the technology underlying the internet. Yet when it comes to producing a steady stream of useful, small-scale innovations, the military often falters. For example, the US military, despite its vast resources, struggled for years to defeat enemies armed with handmade weapons like improvised explosive devices (IEDs), the crude roadside bombs that have injured thousands of US soldiers in the Middle East.

Some of the reasons for this problem are unique to government, including the Pentagon's vast bureaucracy saddled with ultra-complex procurement rules intended to safeguard taxpayers' money. But the biggest challenge is the sheer complexity of developing the kinds of equipment troops need to survive and win battles in the world's most inhospitable places. US soldiers in places like Afghanistan and the Korean DMZ work in conditions that are hard to imagine if you're an engineer or a product designer in a lab or a factory in California or Ohio. The huge gap between the customer and the supplier is one of the main reasons that innovating for the military is an especially difficult challenge.

Today the Pentagon is taking steps to narrow that gap. One strategy it's using: military exercises that simulate real-world conditions in order to test new weapons and other equipment while they are still experimental.

Tech Warrior Enterprise was originally launched as an annual exercise conducted by the Air Force Research Laboratory. In 2018, it was expanded into a year-round program administered by Wright State University's National Center for Medical Readiness, which operates a 52-acre "tactical training site" in Fairborn, Ohio, that's known as "Calamityville." This venue, where all sorts of hazardous events and environments can be simulated, lets civilian engineers and scientists working for startup companies share the battlefield with actual soldiers. The goal is to enable these business leaders to get a firsthand view of how the world looks to the people who will someday be their customers—the American fighting forces that rely on innovative equipment for survival in some of the most dangerous circumstances imaginable.

Tech Warrior Enterprise conducts CONNECT events throughout the year, in which one-on-one assistance is provided to small businesses that are suppliers to the Pentagon. But the biggest event of the year is Operation Tech Warrior, held every fall, which brings a collection of business managers, scientists, and engineers together for an intensive learning experience. They receive two weeks of training and then form a squadron to be led by experienced instructors through a series of operational scenarios, which let them see just how well the gear they're developing works—or doesn't work.

The new kinds of equipment that get their trial by fire in Tech Warrior exercises include tools like infrared markers for nighttime communications, a human motion tracker that can provide GPS positioning even indoors or in an underground tunnel, and a microclimate cooling system designed to be incorporated into a soldier's body armor. These are all products intended for use in extreme conditions, whose effectiveness may spell the difference between victory and defeat for a military unit doing battle with a determined enemy.

As explained by Kristen Barrera, exercise director of Operation Tech Warrior, these "field insertion" activities are designed to help businesspeople understand the real needs of their customers. "It's about exposing them to how our warfighters think," she says. The companies "are building these really cool things, but maybe if they designed [their inventions] just a little bit different, [they] would be more useful in the field. . . . Everything you see during the event is a real military device. The Warriors carry real weapons."[1]

The companies that send team members to join these unique war games consider them invaluable. Mark Tierney is an executive with Eccrine Systems, an Ohio-based company that has been working on wearable, noninvasive electronic devices for monitoring dehydration levels of people under stress, whether they are world-class athletes competing in the Olympics or American soldiers on a desert in the Middle East. Eccrine Systems employees worked closely with Defense Department experts on the design of their devices, but they say they've learned more from participating in two annual Tech Warrior events. "Tech Warrior is a great vehicle for small companies, like ours, to come in and get that end-user feedback under conditions we can't possibly re-create back at the office," Tierney says. "If we can survive here, we can survive out in the real world."[2]

Operation Tech Warrior illustrates one key difference between a company's execution engine and its innovating engine. When your people are working for the execution engine, they generally take a *supplier-side view* of their work. They focus on solving problems that arise when manufacturing products, designing services, and delivering goods to customers; they examine the marketplace and the challenges posed by competitors from their own perspective as suppliers.

By contrast, when your people switch to working for the innovating engine, they need to take a *customer-side view* of their work. They must try to look at potential products and services the way customers might see them—as ways to solve customer problems, satisfy customer desires, and excite customer imaginations.

They must also broaden their perspective to include current *noncustomers*. This includes a broad array of people in various categories, including people who don't patronize the organization today but who might be interested in new products or services that the organization may offer in the future; people from other industries that may offer instructive experiences and insights; and many other people who have unique and potentially valuable knowledge about the marketplace and the needs of customers, including wholesalers and distributors, suppliers of goods and services, members of regulatory bodies and industry groups, social and environmental activists with an interest in business policies, academic experts and researchers, and more. All these different types of noncustomers can play a crucial role in helping you generate innovative ideas that can create big new flows of value for your existing customers, for new customers, and for your organization.

Breaking out of the supplier-side view and learning to think like customers, noncustomers, and potential customers makes innovative thinking much easier—which is why it's important to *everyone* in your organization to master this mode of perception.

Hearing and Heeding the Customer: Easier Said Than Done

It might seem as if the idea of paying attention to customer needs is obvious. There's certainly no shortage of books, articles, seminars, workshops, and training programs that teach concepts like *customer engagement, customer-centricity,* and *customer intimacy.* But actually building your innovating program around the customer-side view of your business is surprisingly difficult. As a result, too many organizations pay lip service to customer closeness while failing to do the work required to overcome the many barriers that make it hard to achieve. The barriers include:

▸ *Insulation from customers:* In most organizations, the higher managers rise in the hierarchy, the less direct contact they have with customers. Thus, those with the greatest power to influence a company's policies—and to shape its innovating program—are often those with the lowest level of current understanding of customer needs and preferences.

▸ *Success-driven inertia:* A company with a track record of success—for example, years of increasing revenues and profits—tends to develop an understandable sense of pride in its accomplishments. Too often, this sense of pride morphs into complacency, with company leaders assuming that the success they've achieved in the past will automatically continue in the future.

▸ *The not-invented-here syndrome:* Many business leaders are reluctant to embrace ideas from outside sources, based in part on the assumption—which may be correct!—that they themselves know more about their industry than other people. They forget that sometimes an outsider with modest technical knowledge may come up with a powerful product or service concept that an insider might never conceive.

▶ *The silence of the customer:* When a company surveys its current customers, they can usually describe what they like or don't like about existing goods or services—important data, no doubt. But they are rarely able to describe or even imagine the kinds of goods and services that *don't* currently exist, but which they would eagerly embrace if they were offered. Helping customers to articulate needs they don't fully understand is a challenging art that few businesses have mastered.

▶ *Failure to consider noncustomers:* Most organizations devote enormous time and energy to serving their current customers well—as they should. But in the process, they lose sight of the countless people they never encounter because they are *not* current customers. Discovering and learning from noncustomers of many kinds takes an imaginative leap that most businesspeople never attempt.

▶ *Fear of cannibalization:* When business leaders discover or learn about a new product or service that customers might like, they are often reluctant to develop it for fear it might steal sales and profits away from their existing offerings. This is especially common when the proposed new product or service could be cheaper or more efficient than the existing good, which means lower profit margins for the business. Leaders who fear cannibalizing their own business are tempted to turn a deaf ear to the needs of customers.

These and other barriers to hearing and heeding the voices of customers help to explain why so many companies fail to consistently develop innovations that are truly customer-centered. For most businesspeople, the path of least resistance is to disregard, deny, or distort the voices of customers rather than pay attention to them. That's why it's important to adopt practices and policies that will force you to remain in close contact with customers and to learn from the messages they send you.

Overcoming Barriers to Innovation: How Ecocem Learns from Customers and Noncustomers

Several of the barriers to adopting the customer-side view—as well as some ways that those barriers can be overcome—are illustrated by the story of Ecocem, a highly innovative company in a relatively little-known industry.[3]

Concrete is one of the oldest and most important building materials known to humankind. Ancient civilizations from the Middle East, Egypt, Greece, Rome, and Mayan Mexico built grand structures with concrete, some of which survive to this day. In general terms, the formula for concrete is simple. It's made by combining aggregate—a mixture of various materials that may include sand, gravel, and crushed stone—with water and cement into a fluid mixture that hardens over time. When it's first mixed, the concrete mixture is easily poured and molded into shape. But after it hardens, it's as solid and durable as stone.

Cement, then, is a key ingredient in making concrete. Made in giant furnaces called kilns, cement is a mixture of various materials such as limestone, clay, shale, and gypsum that are heated and ground into a powder that can be mixed with water. Today's cement industry is an important component of the worldwide construction business, involved in practically every big infrastructure project, from roads, dams, bridges, and airport runways to office buildings and apartment complexes. And because cement is generally considered a commodity product, varying little from one maker to the next, the cement industry has come to be dominated by a handful of giant companies that take advantage of economies of scale to stabilize prices and control the market.

The oligopolistic nature of the cement industry discourages innovation. After all, if your company is one of a handful of firms with a large, stable share of the industry, why mess with a good thing? All you need to do is to keep manufacturing the same product that has been used successfully for centuries, and the customer orders—and the profits—are likely to keep rolling in.

And yet the need for innovation in today's cement industry is real. One of the big reasons is the looming challenge of climate change. The technology of cement manufacturing involves releasing CO_2 from limestone and is highly energy-intensive, so much so that it accounts for an estimated 8 percent of the world's greenhouse gas emissions. This giant carbon footprint means that cement makers are under increasing pressure to develop new materials and methods that reduce emissions and thereby contribute to the worldwide effort to combat climate change.

Unfortunately, large, successful businesses aren't always quick to respond to the pressures exerted by environmental trends. The world's giant cement makers are a case in point. Since the mid-nineteenth century, they've derived most of their revenues and profits from the sale of Portland cement, a specific type of cement developed by British manufacturers and perfected in the decades since then. It's a versatile and highly lucrative product that cement makers are very comfortable with and reluctant to abandon. So rather than search for new formulas and processes that might disrupt their successful businesses, cement industry leaders have delayed responding to the climate change problem. They've generally assumed that, someday, they will have to invest billions in a long-term solution such as carbon capture and storage, which is likely to be imposed on the industry as a whole by government action. Meanwhile, however, they are simply hoping to put off the day of reckoning for as long as possible.

As you can see, the cement industry illustrates vividly some of the barriers that prevent companies from seeing the customer-side view of their business. Cement customers such as construction companies, government agencies charged with developing infrastructure projects, and real estate development firms are all aware that, eventually, a solution to the carbon-emission problem must be found. But meanwhile, it's easier and more profitable for cement makers to ignore that message.

Ecocem is charting a different course. Founded and led by Irish entrepreneur Donal O'Riain, it's a small but rapidly grow-ing cement maker based on an underused innovation: a variant formula for making cement that incorporates blast furnace slag, a by-product of steel manufacture. The Ecocem process uses slag to create what's known as ground granulated blast furnace slag (GGBS), a high-quality cement substitute with a much smaller carbon footprint. The manufacture of GGBS also emits virtu-ally no toxic pollutants, and the concrete that incorporates it is especially strong and durable. Today, Ecocem is producing GGBS in three European countries, especially in France, where its latest and largest manufacturing facility was launched in 2019 in partnership with the Luxembourg-based steel company ArcelorMittal.

Ecocem exists because O'Riain heard a customer message that others in the cement industry had chosen to disregard. The environmental and other benefits offered by its main product were enough to help the company get off the ground. But indus-try barriers made it hard for Ecocem to expand as quickly as O'Riain would have liked. It's tough to convince customers to buy a new, unfamiliar product—even one that promises to solve a problem that customers themselves are well aware of—when the big incumbent businesses that dominate the industry all pooh-pooh your new offering.

Another barrier is the fact that the construction industry is heavily regulated. That's understandable, since the strength and safety of buildings, roads, bridges, and other infrastructure projects is a matter of life and death. But, as a result of strict regulation, industry rules, norms, and practices tend to be rigid and difficult to change. And, of course, making changes is especially difficult when those changes are opposed by big, powerful industry players like the leading members of the cement oligopoly.

Faced with these barriers, Ecocem realized that building a profitable, growing business in response to the customer message about the ecological problems with cement would require additional innovative steps. One of these was learning to listen to industry regulators—an important and influential noncustomer group—and finding ways to work with them.

In response to this challenge, O'Riain and his business team responded with action on several fronts. They spent time communicating with members of the committees and boards that establish industry norms, and they urged these groups to include experts who understood the value of GGBS cement and supported its use. Gradually, these outsider voices managed to make themselves heard. After four years of what O'Riain describes as "a pitched battle," the French regulatory committee that governs construction product rules approved GGBS cement as a high-quality substitute for Portland cement in a wide range of building applications. This opened up a significant slice of the market to Ecocem.

At the same time, O'Riain realized that Ecocem would need to get even closer to customers to ensure that it was meeting their needs as fully as possible. He knew that cement customers cared about the greenhouse gas problem—but he didn't yet know what it would take to convince those customers that GGBS cement should be part of the solution.

In response to this challenge, O'Riain began building an innovating team within Ecocem that could listen to customers, understand their needs, and develop ways to make the company's products and services even more attractive and useful. In 2012, he hired a sophisticated and creative materials expert named Laurent Frouin to head this innovating team. Then Ecocem made agreements with two French universities that were already leaders in materials science research under which the company would finance doctoral degree studies for selected students. After they earned their PhDs, these young scientists became part of Frouin's innovating team. Eight years later, Frouin's team now includes a dozen of the brightest and most creative materials science experts in the entire cement industry.

Perhaps most important, O'Riain has taken steps to ensure that this team of scientists has unusual access to the voices of Ecocem's customers. He started sending members of the innovating team out on the road in partnership with Ecocem's salespeople to visit customers as well as noncustomers with the potential to be converted into customers. Together, they would discuss customer needs and explore the kinds of products and services customers would find most helpful.

There was some initial skepticism that this collaboration between salespeople and scientists would work. But it quickly proved to be invaluable. The customers were surprised and delighted to have a chance to meet with leading experts from the world of materials science, and they were fascinated to learn more about the benefits of Ecocem's offerings. The salespeople were proud to be able to show off the advanced technical expertise that Ecocem was developing. And the scientists from Ecocem's innovating team gleaned insights into the needs and preferences of customers that they'd never have encountered back in the lab.

Teaming up salespeople with technology experts was a win/win/win solution that also went a long way toward overcoming one of the big barriers many companies face when they seek to understand customer needs—namely, the isolation of would-be business innovators from the customers they seek to serve.

Thanks to the deep and ever-expanding connections between Ecocem's customers and its innovating experts, Ecocem has been developing new solutions that produce enormous value for customers while opening up new markets for the company and its products. Here's one example.

A government agency in Sweden charged with redeveloping the infrastructure of a cargo port at the city of Gävie came to Ecocem with a problem. During dredging, it had discovered that the sediment under the port had been badly contaminated with dangerous deposits of cadmium and other heavy metals from a previous era of industrialization. Could Ecocem find a way to make it possible for this soil to be incorporated safely into land reclamation?

The scientists from Ecocem spent four years and invested some €600,000 (equivalent to more than $700,000) in working on the problem with local experts. They eventually found a way to use Ecocem's GGBS technology to capture and stabilize the heavy metals so that the redeveloped port would be safe from leaching pollutants. Profits from the project have more than earned back the total that Ecocem spent on its research—and now additional projects are emerging to which the same heavy-metals solution can be applied. A new niche market serving customers who otherwise might never have done business with Ecocem is now being created.

The creative partnership among Ecocem's scientists, its sales-people, and the company's customers has paid off for everyone. It's a great example of what can happen when a company works hard to hear and heed the perspectives of customers—even in a tradition-bound industry that sometimes throws up barriers to innovation.

Cocreating with Customers and Other Stakeholders

One of the best ways to develop and deepen your customer-side view of the business is to create a space and a set of processes for working in partnership with customers, key noncustomers, and others from outside your business. The Pentagon's Operation Tech Warrior is one example. Another is the Innovation Center in Silicon Valley run by W. L. Gore, the fabric technology company profiled in Chapter 2.

As we've discussed, W. L. Gore's gift for innovation is nurtured largely by its Dabble Time policy, which encourages employees throughout the business to spend time and energy creating and exploring new ideas. But many companies find that relying on self-generated ideas is not enough to keep their businesses growing and evolving. Founded in 2017, the Innovation Center is Gore's way of partnering with innovators from a wide range of organizations—customers, academic researchers, startup entrepreneurs, corporate suppliers, and others—to develop value-creating concepts that Gore alone might not have conceived.

The Innovation Center is an 11,000-square-foot facility that includes a prototyping lab equipped with everything from laser cutters and 3D printers to advanced machinery for microscopy and wet chemistry. Here Gore engineers and scientists work hand-in-hand with outside experts to develop and test new product ideas. The same space is also used for special events, dubbed "hackathons" and "make-a-thons," in which outside guests are invited to play with ideas for new applications of Gore's many existing products. Finding such new applications and launching businesses built around them has been one of Gore's most important forms of innovation and a source of enormous growth.

The work done at the Innovation Center is far from random. Instead, it is focused on specific areas of technology that Gore has identified as particularly important for its future growth. For example, during 2020–2021, the studies at the center were centered on technologies that include bioelectronics, sustainable fabrics, and neurostimulation (a medical technique that can be used to restore function to patients suffering from paralysis or sensory losses). For each of these technology areas, Gore is working with customers, suppliers, and other stakeholders to discover new ways it can apply its materials expertise to solving problems.

Paul Campbell, who helps run the Innovation Center, explains the intensive process whereby Gore cocreates with customers. It begins with a deep-dive conversation in which engineers, designers, and other experts from both companies engage in an open-ended exploration of the customer's goals, constraints, and unmet needs. Then a sophisticated software tool is deployed to help determine whether or not Gore has a product that might meet the customer's needs:

> Gore's catalog of materials, fabrics, sensors, and other technologies is so vast that no one person has a full grasp on everything that the company has to offer. In order to work around that challenge, . . . software developers created an AI [tool] that can analyze the needs of a particular client, scan the Gore product database for the best options available, and recommend solutions to fit their specific needs. Once that information is provided, the client can then work directly with Gore engineers and designers to see if the products that the AI [tool] selected are a good fit and make sense for the particular application.[4]

If it turns out that the existing Gore product line doesn't have a material that's a perfect fit for the customer need, scientists from the two companies may work together to develop a new variation that can solve the customer's problem—and perhaps create a significant new market for Gore.

One example of how the Innovation Center empowers Gore to learn from customers is the company's ongoing collaboration with Moray Medical, a company that uses robotics technology to improve so-called transcatheter mitral valve procedures, which can be used to replace risky and invasive open-heart surgery for patients with damaged heart valves. Moray Medical's intimate connection with its own healthcare customers—patients, physicians, technical experts—lets it work with Gore's materials experts to develop therapeutic techniques that Gore alone could never have devised. Thus, the center is a venue in which learning from Gore's customers—and those customers' customers—is facilitated and enhanced, to the benefit of all parties.

The cocreation activities fostered in the Innovation Center are one way that Gore strives to ensure that the innovative ideas being produced by the company's scientists and engineers are relevant to the needs of customers. Others include "innovation days" conducted on-site at customer facilities, as well as frequent working sessions that bring together Gore's market-facing professionals with members of the research and development team. Activities like these create close, continuing connections between Gore's frontline innovators and the outside world they seek to serve.

In my years as a consultant and trainer helping companies to strengthen their innovating engines, I've observed a number of important and hopeful trends. One is a growing willingness of businesses to collaborate closely with other companies on innovating projects. In some cases, the innovating partners are customers, like the customers with whom Gore collaborates in its Innovation Center, or the customers like Adidas and Procter & Gamble that BASF has partnered with.

In other cases, companies develop an innovating ecosystem by partnering with outside startups or suppliers to develop new ways of creating value for customers and for themselves. One successful program of this kind is Paint the Future, an initiative created by the Dutch-based firm AkzoNobel, which specializes in paints and performance coatings of many kinds. I conducted my first training program with AkzoNobel in 2009. It led to six more programs involving a total of 150 employees across several business units, and I've followed the company's development with interest ever since.

Paint the Future is an open innovation platform that invites outside companies—in some cases, startups—to address a business challenge defined by Klaas Kruithof, the chief technology officer of AkzoNobel, and his supporting team. The 20 most attractive concepts that surface are selected for further development, including a one-week workshop at AkzoNobel at which the members of the startup company get advice and coaching to improve their idea from a range of AkzoNobel experts. Then three to five winners are selected to collaborate with AkzoNobel. In addition to generating valuable innovative ideas, a goal of Paint the Future is to help build promising startup companies into successful businesses that can be important long-term partners within AkzoNobel's broader business ecosystem.[5]

Many of today's business challenges are too complex for a single company to solve on its own. Cocreating with other companies in your business ecosystem can be an effective way to bring together the ideas, skills, contacts, and other resources needed to produce truly powerful innovations.

Customers (and Noncustomers) Take Many Forms: How an Innovative Nonprofit Builds Stronger Links with Donors

As I noted in the Introduction, when it comes to innovation, the term *customer* should be understood in the broadest possible sense. *Everyone* in your organization has a customer, either an internal or external one. For example, an employee in the human resources department creates value for internal customers that may include fellow employees (who may be served with career counseling or training programs) and senior management (who may be served with the design of a new succession planning system). Innovating is about seeking ideas for creating new value for *any* of these customers.

Defining customers (and noncustomers) broadly is an important innovation strategy for all sorts of organizations. Consider charity: water, a nonprofit organization dedicated to bringing clean, safe drinking water to people all over the world. One set of customers that charity: water serves is the families in rural villages who rely on the organization for access to potable water. However, another, less-obvious set of individuals whose voices are also important to charity: water is the donors who provide the nonprofit with the money that makes its work possible.

Donors to a nonprofit like charity: water aren't customers, since they don't purchase products or services as customers do. But they do give their money to the organization in exchange for "goods" of a different kind—namely, the sense of satisfaction and pride that comes from knowing that their contributions have helped make life better for the people whom charity: water serves. If that psychological and emotional benefit is delivered in a powerful, compelling fashion, the donors are likely to continue contributing. If not, the money will dry up, and charity: water may be forced to shut its doors. Thus, the relationship between these noncustomers and the charity: water team has much in common with the customer–supplier relationship—and is arguably at least as important.

To better serve this vital noncustomer group, charity: water has enhanced its donor engagement program in a number of innovative ways. For example, it created its Dollars to Projects program, which provides donors with "completion reports" on every project they've helped to fund, including pictures, results data, GPS coordinates, and even live video from sites in African villages or Latin American farms. The goal is to provide the "wow experience" of seeing firsthand the impact of their gifts that intensifies and deepens the bond between the donors and the organization they support.

Another innovation has been the creation of a two-track funding mechanism that separates overhead from direct programming expenditures. Overhead costs such as staff salaries, office space, and fundraising expenditures are covered by a small group of wealthy donors who are known as The Well. Drawn largely from the philanthropic community in Silicon Valley—a network of people who have been assiduously cultivated by Scott Harrison, the founder of charity: water—the 133 members of

The Well each donate between $60 thousand and $1 million. This allows the organization to tell smaller donors that every dollar they give will go directly to program costs. It's a fundraising model that enhances the appeal of charity: water for ordinary givers. And while some nonprofit experts consider the message this sends to be slightly misleading (since it suggests that other nonprofits are somehow less efficient than charity: water), the same two-track funding has been adopted by a number of other nonprofits, such as Episcopal Charities of New York.

Members of The Well benefit from an even more intensive donor engagement program. Many are invited to travel to Africa with founder Harrison, where they get to see firsthand the work their gifts make possible. "It gives you the chills and makes you feel great," said one executive after a 2019 trip to Ethiopia. "There's nothing like seeing in real life what it's like to bring water to a real community," said another.[6]

On top of all this, charity: water has also enhanced the donor experience by sharing an unusually extensive trove of information with its financial supporters. It has been given the coveted "Platinum Seal of Transparency" by Candid, the information service that rates over 2.5 million nonprofit organizations for their commitment to openness in providing information about their work, their finances, and even the mistakes they commit.

Thanks to its deep understanding of the perspective of donor-customers, the team at charity: water has been able to create stronger, more long-lasting bonds with those donors, making the organization's lifesaving work more sustainable. As of 2019, the organization has raised more than $370 million and says that its wells have brought clean drinking water to over 10 million people. Scott Harrison has ambitious growth plans for the years to come. Continuing to be an innovator in connecting effectively with donor-customers may help him achieve his goals.

The lesson of this chapter is clear, and it's one that applies to every kind of organization. To keep your innovating engine humming, everyone in the organization must be trained to periodically pivot his or her mindset or mental frame away from the dominant supplier-side view of the business and adopt instead the customer-side view.

KEY TAKEAWAYS FROM CHAPTER 3

- When running the execution engine, employees typically take a *suppler-side view* of their work. By contrast, the innovating engine demands a *customer-side view.*
- Every employee needs to learn to understand the customer-side view of your business—which includes the perspective of *noncustomers* who may be converted into customers as well as others with unique insights into the market and the best ways to serve it.
- Learning to hear and heed the messages from customers isn't easy. There's an array of psychological and organizational barriers that commonly make it hard for leaders to truly understand and act upon their customers' perspectives. Be aware of these barriers, and develop processes to break them down.
- Be sure to define both "customers" and "noncustomers" as broadly as possible. Include both *internal* and *external customers* and anyone who is served by the work you do. This definition expands the field for potential innovations as widely as possible.

PART TWO

THE THREE KEY PROCESSES OF INNOVATING

4

THE THREE PROCESSES OF INNOVATING

CREATION, INTEGRATION, REFRAMING

So far in this book, I've explained why your organization needs to operate simultaneously in two ways—as an execution engine and as an innovating engine. The execution engine serves your existing customers with products and services that meet their current needs as best as possible, while the innovating engine prepares you to serve the emerging needs of those customers as well as the needs of customers you do not yet know. The execution engine is about your company's present, while the innovating engine is about its future. And while these two engines do different things and operate in different ways, they should not be made up of separate teams unconnected to one another. In fact, everyone in your organization should contribute to the work of *both* engines. This is the best way to ensure that both the execution engine and the innovating engine will have access to the finest talents, ideas, energies, and other resources your organization has to offer.

In addition, I've shown that one key distinction between the execution engine and the innovating engine is the point-of-view characteristic of each. In most organizations, the execution engine tends to have an inside-out, company-centric perspective, focused on managing internal processes as efficiently, accurately, and profitably as possible. Your innovating engine should purposefully adopt a different perspective, one that is outside-in and customer-centric. Only by deeply understanding the interests, needs, dissatisfactions, and wishes of customers—both those you currently serve and those who could become your customers in the future—can you imagine the kinds of innovations that will create new value for those customers as well as for your organization.

Now, having laid this groundwork for understanding how you need to think about innovation, let's delve more deeply into the practical steps involved in building a great innovating engine and making it run as powerfully and productively as possible.

As mentioned in the Introduction, your company's innovating engine is driven by three key processes: *creation, integration, and reframing* (see Figure 4.1).

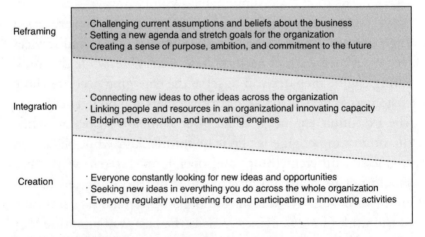

Reframing
· Challenging current assumptions and beliefs about the business
· Setting a new agenda and stretch goals for the organization
· Creating a sense of purpose, ambition, and commitment to the future

Integration
· Connecting new ideas to other ideas across the organization
· Linking people and resources in an organizational innovating capacity
· Bridging the execution and innovating engines

Creation
· Everyone constantly looking for new ideas and opportunities
· Seeking new ideas in everything you do across the whole organization
· Everyone regularly volunteering for and participating in innovating activities

FIGURE 4.1   The Three Key Processes of Innovating

Creation is the process by which the organization continuously generates new ideas. And while we most commonly think about innovation in terms of new products, the new ideas that companies need to survive and thrive involve everything they do—not just product design but also customer service, logistics and fulfillment, financial management, human resource (HR) development, information technology, and much more. Consider, for example, the way BASF has developed the capability to innovate not just through inventing new products and services but by modifying the ways it sells those products and services to customers and even adopting new business models that create fresh streams of value both for customers and BASF.

This means that the process of creation can and should take place continually in every department and at every level of your organization. However, many companies find that their frontline employees play the most important role in directly generating new ideas. This is natural, since in most organizations the frontline workers are the ones who have the most direct contact with customers (and noncustomers) and therefore find it easiest to adopt a customer-centric perspective. Frontline workers also have the most hands-on, day-to-day connection with the organization's main processes, from product manufacturing to customer service. So while everyone in your organization should be encouraged to generate new ideas, frontline workers tend to be the most prolific fountains of such ideas. For this reason, I refer to them as *frontline innovators*.

The second process driving the innovating engine is *integration*. It's not enough to have a stream of innovative ideas flowing from your employees. Those ideas also need to be evaluated, selected, supported, developed, and channeled through a system that converts the best new ideas into business initiatives to be carried out by the execution engine. I've described how this works at W. L. Gore, where ideas generated by employees during their Dabble Time are tested by a three-stage review process called "Real, Win, Worth." Ideas that win approval through this process may become the basis of new businesses that attract new customers to Gore and support the organization's long-term growth.

The integration process is also about bringing together all the disparate parts of the organization to help keep the innovating engine humming. For practical reasons, the execution engine tends to operate in siloed fashion, with various departments handling different tasks quite separately from one another. Innovating works best when silos are broken down so that ideas can flow freely among people with diverse backgrounds, skills, and perspectives. Companies that excel at innovating create ways to form multidisciplinary networks that span the entire organization and even include people and groups from outside the organization. This, too, is an element of the integration process.

As with all three innovating processes, integration involves employees from the top to the bottom of the organization. But midlevel managers have an especially crucial role to play in integration. They work directly with frontline employees, guiding and evaluating their work, and therefore have an enormous influence on the degree to which frontline innovators are encouraged and rewarded for innovating. They also have the opportunity to make connections with managers from other departments, which means they can help to facilitate the formation of organizational networks that support innovating. Because these middle managers help to encourage and direct the innovative work of the employees they supervise, I often refer to them as *midlevel coaches*.

The third process of innovation is *reframing*. This process is about taking a fresh look at your organization, its mission, its customer base, its characteristic activities, its strength and weaknesses, and its competitive strategy. It's about asking probing questions about all these features that define the organization: Why have we made the choices we have? Are these choices serving us and our customers well? How are changes in our business environment impacting the value of those choices? What kinds of innovations should we be considering that might help us provide greater value for an evolving world?

Asking questions like these is outside the role of the execution engine. When operating in execution mode, our job is to carry out the existing work of the organization as well as we possibly can, not to challenge or question the decisions that define that work. But probing questions are essential to the work of the innovating engine. The answers you come up with may lead you to fundamentally reframe your organization's future plans and even its basic identity—in which case, your organization itself may end up being reframed.

Reframing is a valuable activity for everyone in your company to participate in, but it's especially central to the work of your top management. These *senior leaders* should be continually looking over the horizon, trying to anticipate changes in the world to which your company may need to respond. Then they should empower and encourage employees throughout the organization to keep the innovating engine humming so that you'll be prepared to face the future.

Triggering Innovation in a Slow-Growing Commodity Business

To understand more about how the three processes of innovating work and interact, let's look at a real-life example.

One of the companies I've worked with for years is Kordsa, part of the Sabancı Group, a giant Turkish industrial conglomerate. Güler Sabancı, who has been called "Turkey's business superwoman" and is regularly listed among the world's most powerful female leaders, is chair and managing director of this empire. When I presented the Blue Ocean innovation techniques to her and a select group of her top executives back in 2009, she immediately grasped their significance. At her request, I ended up training managers from eight Sabancı companies, including the leaders of Kordsa. With 4,500 employees and 12 plants located in countries from Indonesia and Thailand to Brazil and the United States, Kordsa is the world's largest maker of yarn and fabrics used in the manufacture of tires and other industrial products.[1]

The innovation challenge faced by Kordsa was one that many companies will find familiar. In the words of Mehmet Pekarun, then the company's CEO, "We were operating a mature business in an industry where the basic nature of the product—fabrics used primarily in automobile tires—had scarcely changed in decades. For this reason, many people in our organization wondered, 'Why should we bother with innovation?'"

But from his vantage point, Pekarun could see how a stagnant innovating engine was preventing the company from growing. Pekarun had joined the firm in 2006 after working for several years in Erie, Pennsylvania, as a manager for GE's transportation systems division. His stint at GE—then one of the world's most progressive, best-managed, and most innovative corporations—had been an invaluable period of education for Pekarun. He was well prepared to take on the challenge of discovering new avenues of growth for Kordsa.

At the time, an important element of Kordsa's business was a joint venture with Dupont, the global chemical company. Kordsa's management had looked to this joint venture as an entry point for the company into the worldwide tire industry. But this dream had not really materialized, and now the deal with Dupont was coming to an end.

Pekarun was charged with defining a way forward. As he studied Kordsa's circumstances, he realized the company faced two primary challenges. First, the conclusion of the joint venture with Dupont meant that Kordsa would no longer have access to the innovative capabilities generated by Dupont's research and development (R&D) operations. Instead, it would have to rely for innovative ideas on its own R&D department, which at the time was small and lackluster.

Second, the lack of a partnership with a big global company would leave Kordsa stuck between its two largest groups of stakeholders: the giant tire makers like Michelin, Goodyear, and Continental, which were Kordsa's chief customers, and the petrochemical companies, which were Kordsa's chief suppliers. Under pricing pressure from both of these powerful sources, Kordsa had little strategic freedom. Company leaders had become accustomed to squeezing out growth simply through buying capacity—that is, making acquisitions of smaller materials manufacturers—rather than through innovation.

This was an inherently limited strategy that would be unlikely to give Kordsa a chance to break out of its business niche. It was up to Pekarun to find a solution.

In order to develop some upside growth potential for Kordsa, Pekarun decided to launch an innovation program. The goal was to fill the technology void left by the departure of Dupont and then to use the innovations Kordsa might create as the basis for reframing the business. Pekarun wanted to transform Kordsa from a provider of commodity materials—one among many, competing almost exclusively on price—into a unique provider of services and solutions, and a valuable innovation partner to its customers.

Fortunately, Sabancı Holding's chairwoman Güler Sabancı was supportive of Pekarun's ideas. She helped to organize a meeting at which a number of outside consultants offered ideas about how to launch a powerful innovating engine at Kordsa. The result of this consultants' "beauty contest" was that I was selected to help develop Kordsa's innovation program.

In addition, CEO Pekarun decided to name an executive who could serve as a dedicated change agent to spearhead the innovation program. While searching for a person to fill this role, Pekarun heard about Cenk Alper, who was then a manager at Bekhaert, a Belgium-based company that specialized in manufacturing steel wire and related products. Alper was both deeply knowledgeable about technology innovation and highly customer-centric in his thinking—just the combination that Kordsa needed.

When Pekarun and Alper met, they immediately clicked. Alper joined Kordsa, and the two men became a highly effective team that would jointly drive the company's transformation in the years to come.

Under their direction, Kordsa began by investing in a new internal technology center. This provided a hub where the company's small R&D operation could be modernized, expanded, and improved. In its earliest stages, this new innovation center was dedicated to experimenting with new production techniques that shaved percentage points off Kordsa's cost structure—for example, by reducing the amount of energy consumed during the manufacturing of tire fabrics. The Kordsa engineers studied methods used in other industries in search of process improvements they could adopt—for example, the use of air-expanded foam rather than water-based materials for coating the undersides of fabrics, borrowed from the carpet industry, and the use of infrared heating rather than convection furnaces, borrowed from industrial bakers.

As these and other process improvements gave Kordsa a competitive price edge over rival suppliers, the company began to gain a reputation as an industry leader.

To build on this reputation, Alper began spending time with leaders from Kordsa's biggest customers, including such international tire manufacturers as Goodyear, Bridgestone, and Continental. From these conversations, he gleaned insights into the problems Kordsa's customers faced, the unmet needs they hadn't previously expressed, and the ways Kordsa might be able to make their operations easier, cheaper, and more efficient. Alper also began hiring retired executives from the biggest tire makers to serve as consultants to Kordsa—"People who could speak the customers' language," as Alper explains. These "translators" became another source of customer insights, helping to generate additional ideas about things Kordsa could do to create more value for tire makers.

To convert these raw ideas into practical concepts, Kordsa began developing new product prototyping capabilities. This wasn't without controversy. One of the first tools the company needed was a trial spinning line, which could be used to produce new fabric yarns and test their strength, flexibility, and adhesion level. This would require a million-dollar investment, and Alper's request for these funds met some resistance from the company's board. Why spend so much money on a machine that wouldn't even be producing materials for sale to customers? But Alper pushed back, explaining that this was an investment in Kordsa's future. With support from Pekarun, Alper got the funding, and he and his team continued building the R&D capacity that the company really needed.

Within a few years, Kordsa would be operating a state-of-the-art experimental lab that customers themselves could visit, bringing their ideas and watching as Kordsa's engineers worked to implement and test them. Tire manufacturers began to come to Kordsa's engineers with questions about their own internal processes: "We are spending a lot of money on certain stages in the manufacturing process. Is there any way you can help us become more efficient?" Kordsa's scientists started working with customers to cocreate solutions to such challenges.

Little by little, Kordsa transformed itself from a provider of commodity goods—one among many—into a unique provider of services and solutions, and a valuable innovation partner to its customers. One example is a new type of tire cord fabric, branded as Capmax, that eliminates several time-consuming and costly stages in the tire manufacturing process, saving customers money as well as material usage.

This change opened up powerful new growth opportunities for Kordsa. Rather than having to rely on company acquisitions to expand its revenue base, Kordsa now began creating a steady stream of new product and service offerings that it could sell to its existing customers. Gradually Kordsa became more and more important as a supplier to its biggest customers, and claimed a steadily increasing fraction of their spending on materials, components, and services. Michelin raised Kordsa's company ranking from "low-tier supplier" to "strategic supplier," reflecting its enhanced value to the tire maker, and soon other giant tire companies followed suit.

Furthermore, new customers that had never considered Kordsa as a potential supplier also began to pop up on the company's radar, providing still more growth opportunities. These included customers in industries outside of the tire business where reinforced composite materials like the ones Kordsa makes are widely used—for example, construction, aerospace, and electronics. Kordsa found that its technological breakthroughs could be applied to a range of industries, and it opened a new revenue stream based on licensing them to other companies.

Today, Kordsa is considered one of the most innovative companies in Turkey. It's ranked number three in R&D capabilities among all Turkish corporations and has won numerous awards for innovation from groups like the Turkish Export Council and the national Sustainability Council.

Cenk Alper succeeded Pekarun as CEO of Kordsa. Pekarun rose to become a member of the executive committee of the entire Sabancı Group, and his area of responsibility was broadened to include several other companies within Sabancı's Industrials group, including such varied businesses as men's and women's apparel, corrugated packaging materials, and automotive technology. In each case, he instituted a program centered on innovation, with top-down initiatives designed to support the creation of breakthrough ideas on the front lines of the organization and the development and spread of those ideas with the help of midlevel managers. Within five years, the roster of products offered by Sabancı's Industrials group had increased fivefold, and sales for the group had increased by 70 percent.

In April 2017, a former project engineer named Ali Çalişkan, who had held a variety of important technical roles at Kordsa, was elevated to the position of CEO, replacing Alper. Çalişkan's rise was an extension of another innovation-centric policy that Pekarun had pioneered at Kordsa—namely, putting people with deep roots in technological innovation in key leadership roles. Alper, the Kordsa executive who had helped to transform the company, is now the CEO of Sabancı Holding.

Looking back on Kordsa's recent history, Pekarun summarizes the company's transformation this way: "It's fascinating to realize the upside you may have in a mature industry once you get closer to your customers!"

How the Three Processes of Innovating Combined to Transform Kordsa

Now let's take a step back and analyze how the three processes of creation, integration, and reframing worked within Kordsa to turn it into one of Turkey's most innovative companies.

Kordsa's leadership encouraged the process of *creation* by providing workers at all levels of the organization with the tools, resources, and—perhaps most important—the permission they needed to innovate.

After I was hired to serve as Kordsa's consulting expert on innovation, I helped set up training programs that introduced everyone in the company to the Blue Ocean tools for analyzing their business and identifying potential opportunities for innovative growth. Alper and his team then conducted a survey of the organization that identified bright spots where innovation was already happening in a small way, and they made sure that these initiatives were publicly recognized, encouraged, and rewarded.

They also analyzed the entire industry landscape to find "adjacent businesses" where Kordsa was not currently active but where there was the potential for innovation-driven expansion. They hired experts in technical areas where they discovered Kordsa needed to improve its level of knowledge, such as polymer technologies. And they made sure that every business unit within the company had at least one Blue Ocean innovation project to work on, so that the concept of innovating would become widespread in the organization.

All these actions helped fuel an explosion of new innovating ideas as the company's frontline employees, middle managers, and top-level executives all began to think about innovation as part of their daily work.

In the years since Alper began activating Kordsa's innovating engine, the embedding of the creation process throughout the organization has advanced still further. In the mid-2010s, Kordsa instituted a new program it referred to as total productive maintenance (TPM). Its goal is what Alper describes as "the democratization of innovation." Taught to workers at every Kordsa facility, TPM gives every employee the power to design and implement processes that improve their own jobs while creating extra value for Kordsa and its customers.

The result is a constant stream of innovations, some big, some small. Three modest yet illustrative examples:

▸ A clever frontline worker developed a simplified method of changing the oil filter on an assembly-line machine that cuts the time for the task from half an hour to five minutes.

▸ To solve the problem of rolls of packaged fabric moving around while being transported by truck, a worker who rode in the back of the truck came up with the idea of installing airbags to stabilize the load, thereby preventing damage and saving significant expense.

▸ An ingenious human resources employee improved the employee on-boarding and training process by proposing that every new worker be assigned a "buddy." The buddy serves as a guide and mentor for the new employee's first year on the job, answering questions and helping the new team member learn the Kordsa culture. Once implemented, this new system reduced the stress on company

HR managers and trainers, and even led to the creation of a number of lasting friendships. In fact, Kordsa now calls the program "Buddies Forever."

As you can see, embedding the creation process into every corner of Kordsa has led to a remarkable outpouring of many kinds of innovations—not just new product ideas but new process and management ideas that keep making Kordsa a better place to work.

To promote the second innovation process—*integration*—Alper and his team created a number of organizational systems to transform the raw ideas that bubble up from Kordsa's employees into business opportunities that can be acted upon by the company's execution engine. Kordsa employs what's called a *stage-gate system* to organize its innovation activity. This is a project management method in which an innovative concept—for example, a new product idea—is developed through a prescribed series of steps or stages, linked to one another through a sequence of gates. Movement through the gates is controlled by a leadership committee that determines whether or not the concept has met the criteria to make it eligible for the next stage. For example, one gate early in the process requires the building of a convincing business case for the concept; another requires testing and validation of the concept through usage by actual customers; and so on. To protect a promising innovative concept from excessive economic pressures that could squelch it in its early phases, the Kordsa stage-gate system "positively discriminates" in favor of new businesses by exempting them from the corporation's usual profit requirements for their first five years. This gives the fledgling businesses a chance to grow to scale while any flaws in the profit model are being identified and eliminated.

Continuing the integration process, the entire Sabancı Industrials Group of companies also introduced activities that helped spread innovative practices and facilitated connections among innovators across the group. For example, innovation topics were integrated into the group's quarterly meetings. The general manager from one of Sabancı's industrial divisions would bring members of a product team to the meeting to present one of their newest innovation initiatives and respond to comments and questions from colleagues from the other companies.

This practice produced a number of benefits. It promoted the spread of innovative ideas and behaviors from one business unit to another; it established personal connections among innovation-minded employees, which often led to productive meetings and conversations in the future; and it incentivized and rewarded team members for their innovative activities by giving them a prominent internal platform for their work. In some cases, the individual companies' general managers themselves had not been strongly supportive of their team members' innovative projects. By shining a spotlight on those projects in the group's quarterly meetings, the Sabancı group publicly encouraged the team members without doing anything to embarrass or alienate their general managers. This helped spread the entrepreneurial spirit from one business unit to another.

Corporate leaders also employed their personal communication resources to further spread the "innovation contagion." They created a private list of managers within the Industrials group under three headings depending on their attitude toward the innovation initiative—some listed as supporters, some as opponents, and some as undecided. They then implemented a communications strategy for each group, designing emails, memos, presentations, speeches, and other forms of messaging to move each group in the right direction—encouraging and energizing the supporters, responding to the concerns of the opponents, and intriguing and attracting the undecided. To further support the necessary cultural shift, CEO Alper made time in his schedule to personally lead the training sessions in which new employees would learn to use the Blue Ocean innovating tools.

Through these and other steps, the leadership team pushed the corporate culture of Kordsa to become more welcoming to innovation, helping to turn isolated pockets of innovation into a widespread pattern of behavior that everyone understood was normal and necessary. These were all key elements of the integration process.

Finally, Alper spearheaded the *reframing* process for Kordsa. Through words and actions, he taught people throughout the organization, from the managers who reported directly to him to the engineers in the labs and the workers on the factory floors, to think of Kordsa not just as a materials supplier but as a creator of solutions for customers. In effect, Kordsa was reframing its very identity so as to put innovation at its core.

This wasn't an easy task. It involved a number of cultural shifts, some obvious, others more subtle. At first, some managers from departments such as operations and sales pushed back against the new emphasis on innovation. In their work, they routinely faced tough demands for operational efficiency, cost-cutting, and high profit margins—why should the people in R&D be allowed to spend money without having to guarantee results? But of course innovation is all about trying things that are really new—which means that guarantees are impossible.

"We needed to allow people to fail," Alper recalls:

> That meant creating a protective environment for experimentation. I had support for doing that from Mehmet and the board. But at the same time, we raised our overall expectations. We made it clear that innovation was our route to growth, and that we wanted our scientists, engineers, and other workers to be focused on creating new ideas with value-building potential.
>
> We used every tool at our disposal to reinforce the credibility of our R&D efforts. For example, the Turkish government created a regulation saying that any lab that had at least 50 researchers and met some

other criteria could become a certified R&D center. We made sure to meet those requirements, which gave us some prestige and relieved some of the pressure on our organization.

Soon, when Kordsa began to receive awards from independent groups for the quality of our innovations, that helped a lot. It began to transform our brand into one that stood for innovation, and people throughout the company began to realize the value of innovation. They started to take pride in Kordsa's innovative capabilities.

The reframing process that Alper led has now created a new identity for Kordsa. No longer simply a maker of fabrics for auto tires—an undifferentiated supplier of a commodity product—Kordsa has become "The Reinforcer," a technology innovator that can create an ever-expanding range of specialized materials to meet the needs of companies in a wide range of industries, from tires to construction, electronics to aerospace.

Innovation hasn't merely given Kordsa more things to do—it has reframed the company itself.

Today, Alper has risen to the role of CEO of the entire Sabancı group. He has dedicated himself to spreading the culture of innovation and a host of innovating processes throughout the group, to businesses in sectors as varied as concrete, energy, and financial services. He guided the launch of a $30 million corporate venture capital fund that seeks out innovating businesses to invest in, looking particularly for companies engaged in creating new digital and materials technologies that are expected to bring additional value to the current operations of the Sabancı group.

Alper himself teaches a class in innovating methodologies to cross-business groups of midlevel managers. It's a symbolic gesture that leaves no doubt as to the commitment of top leadership to the mission of innovation.

Historic Nonprofit Innovates
to Meet New Challenges

Like for-profit businesses, nonprofit organizations must be willing to engage in the reframing needed to remain hospitable to innovation. Consider the YMCA. Founded in London in 1844 under the name of the Young Men's Christian Association by a department store worker named George Williams, the YMCA was brought to the United States in 1851 by a retired sea captain from Boston named Thomas Valentine Sullivan. Today, the venerable community institution is familiar to most Americans as the place where kids go to shoot hoops or swim a few laps in the pool. But there's much more to the YMCA than this. Over the decades, the Y (as most people now call it) has gone through a series of reframings, repeatedly innovating its service model in response to new social challenges.

In its original incarnation under the direction of George Williams, the Y was a center of study and prayer designed to help young people develop sound moral and intellectual values despite being surrounded by the temptations of the city of London. The core of that mission—helping people develop their own resources and so enjoy more productive, satisfying lives—has remained constant. But new ways of pursuing that mission have continually emerged.

In 1856, in response to the growth of America's immigrant population, the Y in Cincinnati, Ohio, offered the nation's first-known program to teach English as a second language—in this case, for German speakers. During the 1860s, YMCA facilities in American cities began offering safe, affordable housing for young people who had moved from the countryside in search of work. Amenities such as gymnasiums and auditoriums were soon added, and in 1881 a Y staffer in Boston coined the term "bodybuilding" and began leading some of the first exercise classes ever taught. Thus, the YMCA became known as a place where people could maintain their physical fitness despite the restrictions of life in the big city.

Program developers at the Y continued to innovate. In 1891, a YMCA training school in Springfield, Massachusetts, was in search of a lively indoor game for young people to play in winter. Tasked with meeting the challenge, a physical education teacher named James Naismith nailed a couple of peach baskets on opposite walls of a gym and invented basketball. It has since become the world's second most popular sport (trailing only soccer). Once again, the Y had used its innovative capacity to respond to customer needs.

The Y also developed programs specifically designed to meet the needs of particular customer groups. In 1853, Anthony Brown, a formerly enslaved man, founded the first YMCA for African Americans. To this day, the Y has a robust array of programs that cater to the interests of Black Americans, including, for example, Black Achievers, a mentoring program launched at the Harlem branch of the Y in 1971 that has since been expanded to include all kids from minority backgrounds.

In 1903, the Y created an "industrial" department to serve the needs of blue-collar workers like miners, lumberjacks, and railroad workers, and later added programs aimed at refugees needing help to adjust to life in America. During World War II, YMCA staff even worked secretly to provide clubs and activities for Japanese-American youth who were being held in US government internment camps.

All of these innovations were crucial to keeping the Y vibrant and relevant to emerging generations of Americans. But perhaps the most dramatic reframing in the history of the YMCA has taken place within the past decade.

In 2010, the leaders of the Y realized that demographic changes in the United States were once again creating new social needs that their organization could help to meet. As the baby-boom generation moved into its retirement years—the largest and wealthiest such cohort in American history—older Americans with enhanced life expectancies found themselves with more free time for self-development than their parents or grandparents before them. As a result, the fastest-growing segment of YMCA membership was not youngsters or even families with children but rather older adults. And while many of these aging boomers were financially well-off, large numbers of them were suffering from chronic health conditions that prevented them from taking full advantage of the leisure and recreational activities the Y offered. These chronic conditions—diabetes, heart failure, pulmonary disease, and obesity—were often poorly diagnosed and treated because of another challenge of American life: the country's dysfunctional healthcare system, which had left millions of people without easy or affordable access to medical treatment.

In these converging social trends, the Y's executive leadership recognized a new opportunity for innovation. The Y began working with medical experts to develop a first-of-its-kind community-based program of intensive lifestyle interventions—diet, exercise, and counseling—to help older people avoid or reduce the impact of the chronic conditions that afflicted millions of their peers. Among other initiatives, the YMCA participated in research by a trio of experts—pediatrician Aaron Carroll, social psychologist David Marrero, and physician Ron Ackermann—to test whether such interventions, facilitated through face-to-face goal-setting meetings, could have a meaningful impact on rates of diabetes in older adults.

The study, conducted at the Indianapolis YMCA, included more than 3,200 patients and produced dramatic results. One group of participants, who were treated only with medication (metformin, which can lower blood sugar), experienced a 31 percent reduction in the risk of developing diabetes. But the group that participated in a 16-hour lifestyle intervention program enjoyed a 58 percent reduction in their risk—and for those aged 70 or above, the reduction was 71 percent. "The trial was ended early," Dr. Carroll explains, "because the results were so compelling."[2]

This study confirmed that the concept of using lifestyle interventions to combat diabetes was potentially valid. Now the creation process had to be complemented by the integration process, so that the YMCA's execution engine could take the new program and begin carrying it out using the resources of the entire organization.

The biggest challenge was finding a way to translate the experimental protocols into a program the Y could implement. As Dr. Carroll notes, "There was no real-world, widespread mechanism to start the intensive intervention the prevention program required. At $1,475 a patient, it was just too expensive and impractical to run in physician offices." But the community-based facilities of the Y offered a viable alternative. Dr. Carroll describes what happened next: "As the behavioral expert, Mr. Marrero worked with the Y to reshape all 16 core intervention lessons and several maintenance lessons into a group-based format led by instructors who were Y employees. The [cost of the] new intervention was about $205 per person, a fraction of the original cost."

Healthcare experts endorsed the value of the Y's program. Soon the federal government offered to help. Further research had shown that the program could reduce new cases of diabetes by as much as 70 percent, potentially saving America's beleaguered healthcare system billions in long-term costs. In 2009, the Affordable Care Act—sometimes referred to as Obamacare—appropriated funds to the federal Centers for Disease Control and Prevention (CDC) to support the implementation of the National Diabetes Prevention Program by the Y and other community groups.

Meanwhile, in December 2010, as the Diabetes Prevention Program was being rolled out, the Y hired Dr. Matt Longjohn, an expert in chronic disease prevention, as the first physician executive in the organization's 160-year history. The launch of the diabetes program and the hiring of Dr. Longjohn represent crucial steps in the Y's latest self-reframing initiative. Dr.

Longjohn declared, "We hope that 20 to 50 years from now people will look at this moment and say that's when the Y got involved in community health."[3]

To implement the diabetes program, YMCA facilities around the country hire health coaches from local communities, focusing on populations that are at greatest risk, such as people of color. This makes the program more accessible and relatable to those who need it most. The Y also offers versions of the program designed for those who are visually impaired as well as those who are most comfortable using languages other than English.[4] In these ways, the Y is practicing one of the most important principles of effective innovating—keeping a sharp focus on the specific, real-world needs of customers (and relevant noncustomers) and being guided by those preferences as it designs its services.

By 2015, more than 1,300 YMCA locations in 43 states and 186 cities around the country were offering the Diabetes Prevention Program. By 2020, over 64,000 YMCA members had participated in the program, and many more had taken part in parallel programs offered by other community groups based on the Y's original research.

What's more, it seems clear that the program has been generating real benefits. In May 2019, the CDC announced that new diabetes cases had experienced their first-ever decade of decline, falling to 1.3 million in 2017 after peaking at 1.7 million in 2008. "While the causes of the plateau and decrease remain unclear," the CDC said, "researchers suggest that they may be driven in part by increased awareness of—and emphasis on—type 2 diabetes prevention, changes in diet and physical activity, and changes in diabetes diagnostic and screening practices."[5]

The YMCA offers a vivid illustration of how even a venerable nonprofit organization can implement the three processes of innovating as a way of meeting social needs in an ever-changing world. Transforming a local "gym and swim" center into an access point for lifesaving health interventions represents the essence of reframing.

KEY TAKEAWAYS FROM CHAPTER 4

- The work of innovating involves three core processes, each of which requires engagement by employees at every level of your organization.
- The first of the three processes crucial to innovating is *creation,* by which a steady stream of new ideas with the potential to improve your business is generated. Frontline innovators play a crucial role in creation.
- The second process is *integration*, which draws together resources from all parts of the organization to help drive the innovating engine. Integration helps to turn innovative ideas into practical initiatives to be implemented by your organization's execution engine. It also spreads innovative thinking throughout the organization, creating networks of people who support one another in the work of innovating. Midlevel coaches have an especially important role to play in integration.
- The third process is *reframing,* by which your organization reconsiders and, when appropriate, alters the mental and strategic assumptions that define and limit its operations. Reframing changes the organization's view of itself and makes room for the successful implementation of innovative ideas. Senior leaders generally drive the reframing process.

5

ANYONE, ANYTIME, ANYWHERE

INNOVATION IS EVERYONE'S BUSINESS

Americans have an unfortunate tendency to think of "old" as equivalent to "old-fashioned." If you've ever caught yourself thinking this way, you might like to visit the suburbs of Helsinki, Finland, and drop in at the headquarters of Fiskars Corporation. Make your way through the gleaming lobby of glass, steel, and stone, with its eye-catching art installations that resemble modernist sculptures—all built from products made and marketed by Fiskars. Past the space-age reception desk and the high-tech conference areas, you'll find a huge exhibit hall with colorful displays highlighting the stylish home products that Fiskars now offers—glassware, ceramics, cookware, cutlery, and more.

The big surprise: one of Europe's most innovative companies is also one of its oldest. And as the company approaches its 400th birthday, Fiskars and its people are more innovative than ever.

Naturally, innovation at Fiskars is largely about new products. But Fiskars may be even better at innovating new processes—new ways to manufacture, market, sell, and service their products. One big reason: employees at every level of the organization are empowered and encouraged to innovate in every aspect of their work. As a result, all three of the key innovating processes—creation, integration, and reframing—are taking place throughout Fiskars and keeping the company's innovating engine humming.[1]

How Fiskars' Innovating Engine Operates

Fiskars was born in 1649 when Peter Thorwöste, a Dutch merchant, was given a government charter to create a blast furnace and forging operation in the village of Fiskars (now part of the town of Raseborg, Finland). The products made by Fiskars Corporation during its earliest years included nails, wires, hoes, and wheel reinforcements made from wrought iron. In 1832, the business added a cutlery mill, which made knives, forks, and scissors. The last-named item became Fiskars' most distinctive product. The best-known design for Fiskars scissors made its debut in 1967, when prototype pairs were produced with distinctive ergonomic plastic handles in a choice of black, green, red, or orange. Fiskars' employees were asked to vote on their favorite color, and orange won. The color was officially trademarked in 2003, and to this day, many varieties of scissors with "Fiskars orange" handles are prized for their ultra-high quality, durability, and ease and comfort of use.

In recent decades, Fiskars has built on its global reputation as a maker of tools for indoor and outdoor use by expanding into a range of adjacent businesses. Company acquisitions have been part of this strategy. In 2007, Fiskars purchased Iittala, a popular maker of tableware and glassware. In 2013, Fiskars acquired Royal Copenhagen, famous since 1775 for its fine porcelain products; and in 2015, it bought the WWRD group of companies, including such brand names as Waterford, Wedgwood, and Royal Doulton. Today, Fiskars consists of three strategic business units: Vita, which includes the drinkware, tableware, and interior products; Terra, which focuses on gardening and other outdoor activities; and Crea, which offers tools for creativity and crafting, including the famous scissors. With its products available in more than 100 countries, Fiskars' annual revenues are nearly $1.4 billion (2020).

Business acquisitions have not been the only way that Fiskars has expanded its market footprint. Internally driven innovation has also been a crucial part of the company's growth strategy. When I spoke with Thomas Enckell, president of Fiskars' European division, he explained how the company has been implementing the principles of Blue Ocean Strategy, an innovation system that I teach my clients, including the leaders of Fiskars.

"The concept of the value curve," Enckell said, "has been a valuable tool for us in analyzing the needs of our customers." (The value curve is a simple diagram that shows how to study the characteristics of a product or service offering in relation to the qualities that customers value.) Enckell went on to explain:

> The value curve concept has also helped us enormously in getting to know *noncustomers*—people who don't currently use Fiskars products but who could become our customers in the future. What's more, studying the product qualities that noncustomers say they are seeking has helped us understand how to innovate in ways that our customers may also value. For example, we've learned a great deal by listening to the ways professional gardeners evaluate

our outdoor tools—pruning shears, axes, spades,
rakes, and the like—even though professional gardeners make up just about 10 percent of our market.
Their preferences have a kind of halo effect on our
offerings: when professionals use our tools, nonpro-
fessionals are encouraged to see them as the best
in the world, which supports our consumer sales
efforts. We've also learned a lot by studying professionals in markets that we don't serve, looking for
common traits. For example, watching and speaking
with surgeons as they use and evaluate cutting tools
like scalpels has given us insight into ways we can
improve the shears and knives we make for use in
the kitchen.

Other professional noncustomers whom Fiskars studies and
learns from include forestry workers, tractor users, and workers
on flower-growing farms. "They use tools like the ones Fiskars
makes all day long and at large scale," says Petteri Masalin, vice
president of Design for Fiskars. "That means they are even better
sources of information about the job to be done with our tools
than the amateur users who typically buy our products."

As you can already see, Fiskars approaches innovation in a
highly methodical fashion. A vivid example is the story behind
one of the company's most successful breakthrough offerings—
the Waterwheel, which was Fiskars' first entry into the highly
competitive marketplace for garden watering equipment.

Masalin—known to his friends as "Pepe"—shared some of
the details of this story with me. In the process, I learned that
the world of watering tools—hoses and irrigation equipment for
use in home gardens—is far from simple.

Before Fiskars decided to take the plunge into this challenging business arena, Pepe and his team engaged in extensive
research. They came to understand many of the complexities
faced by customers seeking the right equipment for using water

in their gardens. Some were unexpected but obvious upon reflection—for example, the fact that varying soil types have differing water absorption characteristics that call for equipment capable of delivering moisture at varying rates. (The soil in southern Europe is much dryer than in Scandinavia, which means it takes much longer to get flower beds fully saturated in a Spanish garden than in a Finnish one.)

Other discoveries posed different design challenges—such as the fact that homeowners find themselves adapting their watering equipment for a range of purposes that have nothing to do with gardening. "People use their hoses to wash their bikes or their boats, to spray down their dogs, and to help their kids cool off in the summertime," Masalin told me. A watering tool that sought to capture a large share of the market ought to be better than the competition at fulfilling all these functions and more. It ought to be easy and reliable to use, unlike many traditional hoses, which are awkward to handle, are difficult to wind and unwind, and have connections that are prone to leaking and breaking. Finally, it should be simple, attractive, and graceful in its appearance—qualities of Nordic design that have long been characteristic of products made by Fiskars.

In Masalin's view, Fiskars had one big advantage over its competitors—namely, the fact that watering was a brand-new category for Fiskars. "The others in this market have been making hoses and related tools for decades," he said. "They are accustomed to their traditional ways of thinking, which makes it hard for them to imagine new designs." Fiskars broke through those conventions. Rather than using the familiar wall-mounted rack on which a hose may be stored, the Waterwheel is an all-in-one device, fitted with wheels, that contains a hose neatly coiled inside it. The user carries the whole kit by its handle and places it horizontally on the ground wherever it will be used.

The user then attaches the inlet hose to the nearest tap, using threaded connectors made of FiberComp, an advanced composite of fiberglass in a thermoset polymer matrix that Fiskars originally developed for use in its axe handles. The FiberComp connectors are extremely light, very strong, resistant to leakage, free of corrosion, and, in chilly weather, much more comfortable to handle than metal.

Now the Waterwheel is ready to use. The 360-degree range of movement it offers makes it easy to spray water in any direction over even a very large home garden. Simple accessories included in the package, like the sprayer support, allow the system to be applied to other uses, such as irrigating a particular spot for a long period of time or setting up a play area for the children on a scorching summer afternoon.

In short, the design that Masalin's team came up with featured a range of remarkable innovations, all based on the deep customer insights that Fiskars had gathered.

In 2016, an early version of the Waterwheel design was sent to a factory in Poland for manufacturing at a small scale, after which it was test-marketed in Finland for a year. The results were so good that the Waterwheel was soon introduced to markets across Europe. It went on to win a number of design prizes, including the prestigious Red Dot award, presented by an international jury annually since 1955. (Fiskars has been recognized repeatedly by the juries that select Red Dot winners. Most recently, in 2020, the design team headed by Masalin— Pepe—was honored by Red Dot as Design Team of the Year, and Fiskars joined Apple, Ferrari, and Adidas as one of the companies in the Hall of Fame established by Red Dot in 1988.)[2]

Today, the Waterwheel line of products has been expanded to include several models, with improved materials and new features continually being added. It's a great example of the systematic innovation process that has helped to make Fiskars such a successful organization.

Of course, as I've emphasized throughout this book, innovation is not just about creating new products like the Waterwheel—important as that is. It's also about creating new ways to serve customers of every kind as well as improved processes that make your organization more efficient, successful, and valuable. Fiskars offers a number of remarkable examples of these kinds of innovations. Here's the story of one.

Outdoor tools made by Fiskars have long been popular staples at every leading gardening center and hardware store in dozens of countries around the world, especially in Europe. But for a long time, the way Fiskars products were displayed, merchandised, and sold was haphazard, confusing, and inefficient.

Merchandising expert Oliver Zehme joined Fiskars in 2014. In his previous career, he'd worked on marketing fast-moving consumer goods like those sold in drugstores and supermarkets. He built on this experience as he set out to work with retailers and his new colleagues to remedy the shortcomings of Fiskars' in-store marketing programs.

"A garden center isn't the same as a supermarket," Zehme concedes. "But many of the customer behaviors are similar. And we realized that if we redesigned the store displays to take those behaviors into account, we could sell a lot more products." Zehme set to work creating a new organizational group within Fiskars—a series of Go-To-Market units, each serving a particular geographic market, such as Europe. In each market, the Go-To-Market team would study consumer expectations, interests, and behaviors, and use these to develop unique merchandising systems that would serve those customers better.

At first, Zehme experienced pushback from a handful of his colleagues at Fiskars, who had difficulty understanding why the way products were organized and displayed was so important. "A few people looked at me as if I was from Mars," he recalls. "They thought I was interested in making the store shelves look more pretty. What a waste of time!"

To demonstrate that rethinking Fiskars' approach to merchandising could generate real value for both the company and its business partners, Zehme and his team started by spending time analyzing how customers bought outdoor tools. Through visits, observations, interviews, and focus groups, they developed some fundamental understandings of the shopping experience. "People don't really go into a store to buy a spade," Zehme explains. "They go there because they want to do a specific job in their backyard or inside their home. So the store should be arranged to make it easy for them to learn how to do that job and to find what they need to do it."

They also learned a number of more specific facts about tool buyers and their habits—for example, that most shoppers at garden centers are females, which perhaps explains why heavy-duty cutting tools like axes don't sell very well there. (Men in search of chopping tools are much more likely to visit hardware stores instead.) Insights like these gave the team ideas about how to customize their merchandising plans to fit specific categories of retailers—for example, by giving garden centers displays of lighter, easier-to-use cutting tools that could serve as alternatives to axes.

To test their innovative insights, Zehme convinced one of Fiskars' biggest accounts—a garden center near Munich—to collaborate on an experiment. Rather than organizing tools by category, they worked together to create customized displays based around specific tasks—for example, preparing a flower bed for planting or installing a picket fence. All the tools needed for the task would be grouped together, along with complementary products (such as soil and fertilizer for the flower beds) as well as "substitutional" products (such as utility knives and hatchets that could be used in place of an axe or saw). The various tools and products would be arranged visually from left to right in a way that mirrored the steps in the process, from start to finish. Informational displays were created, describing exactly how the homeowner should tackle the task and offering guidance on selecting the most appropriate tools.

Within a month, the first set of innovative displays was unveiled in the Munich store. Zehme dubbed it the Ambassador system. Within three days, 2 other stores from the same garden center chain were demanding the same system, and after a month, all 12 stores in the chain had asked to be included. The next year's sales figures reflected a 50 percent increase in the sell-through of Fiskars products.

This was a significant victory because Germany has long been one of the toughest European marketplaces for Fiskars. (Unlike its home market of Finland, where the Fiskars brand is on everybody's lips, Germany is an ultra-competitive market where many brands from around the world do battle.) The fact that the Ambassador system had made such a splash in the Munich area boded well for its impact across the continent. Sure enough, by 2016, the Ambassador system had been successfully rolled out to more than 1,900 stores all over Europe. Zehme and his team began developing similar innovative programs to enhance marketing for other categories of Fiskars products, such as kitchen tools.

The R&D and design teams at Fiskars do an effective job of innovating new products, much as they've done throughout the company's history. But as the Ambassador story suggests, Fiskars is also an extraordinary innovator when it comes to other business processes. As of 2021, the ideas behind the Ambassador system are being applied to Fiskars' other business units.

Innovating Without Boundaries: The Built to Innovate (BTI) Framework for an Innovating Engine

A close look at how innovating happens at Fiskars illustrates the fact that the three processes of innovating don't occur in isolation from one another, nor do they necessarily fit into a neat sequence or system. Creation, integration, and reframing may often occur simultaneously, overlapping and influencing one another. They may also take place—indeed, they *should* take place—in every company department and at every level of the organization.

My study of how such innovation-centered companies operate helped me to develop the framework depicted in the Introduction to this book. For your convenience, we repeat it here, as Figure 5.1. It's a three-by-three framework that illustrates how all three levels of an organization can participate in all three processes of innovating, thereby creating an innovating engine that is operating at maximum efficiency. (An expanded version of the BTI framework with additional information about the processes appears in the Appendix.)

As Figure 5.1 shows, all three processes—creation, integration, and reframing—should be taking place at any given time in each of the three major levels in most organizations. But notice that these processes operate somewhat differently and to varying degrees at each level. Among frontline innovators, the most important process is creation, which mainly takes the form of generating ideas—although frontline innovators take part in integration and reframing as well. Among midlevel coaches, integration is the most important process, although they also participate in creation and reframing. And among senior leaders, reframing is the most important process, though they too are involved in all three processes. In each column of Figure 5.1, the relative size of the cells reflects the degree of importance that each process plays in the work of that group of employees.

Let's use Fiskars as an example of how each of the three core processes of innovating gets played out at each level of a well-run innovating engine.

The creation process, in which a stream of innovative ideas is continuously generated, happens largely at the level of frontline innovators. People who work directly with customers (and noncustomers) often have special insights into customer needs, problems, and wishes, which may trigger ideas for new products or services. Similarly, people directly engaged with hands-on technological or design work—such as engineers, scientists, programmers, artists, packagers, materials experts, and

	Frontline Innovators	Midlevel Coaches	Senior Leaders
Reframing	Look Beyond the Obvious	Give Permission to Innovate; Create a Fair Process	Put Innovation at the Core of Strategy; Allow Challenges to Assumptions
Integration	Share Innovative Practices and Customer Knowledge	Build a Connective Process; Link the Execution and Innovating Engines	Create a Governance Structure and a Language for Innovating
Creation	Generate Ideas by Listening to Customers and Noncustomers	Provide Support; Review and Channel Ideas	Set Norms, Standards, and Incentives for Innovating

FIGURE 5.1 The BTI Framework

Innovation by Anyone, Anytime, Anywhere—How the Three Processes of Innovating Take Place at Three Levels of an Organization

manufacturing specialists—often find that new ideas arise from their daily interactions with products and services the company offers as well as with important noncustomers such as suppliers, researchers, and outside consultants.

This certainly happens at Fiskars. Masalin and his cross-functional design team spent hours observing and talking with customers before they set about creating their innovative design for the Waterwheel system. Similarly, Zehme's ideas that ultimately gave rise to the Ambassador system arose largely through his visits to retailers and his conversations with store managers and salespeople who were directly involved in selling Fiskars products in retail settings.

Similar idea-generating activities take place at the frontline level of Fiskars on a regular basis. Every business unit has what's called a *customer insight group*—an interdisciplinary team of employees whose job is to record and analyze what customers, suppliers, salespeople, and others are saying about shifting market dynamics. Trends and opportunities discerned by the customer insight group members often give rise to new ideas for products, services, or process improvements.

Similar frontline discoveries happen at Fiskars' R&D facilities. These include kitchens, gardens, and workshops that are used not just by Fiskars' own engineers and scientists but by outside professionals who are not typical Fiskars' customers but who use similar kinds of tools—chefs, gardeners, woodworkers, interior designers, and so on. They're invited to work in the Fiskars' facilities, using existing products and testing prototypes of new ones. The members of the Fiskars team observe the professionals in action, noting how the company's products work well (and when they don't), asking and answering questions, and exploring challenges that might suggest ways the Fiskars products could be improved or supplemented. Even its classic scissors continue to be rethought and improved through this process, with variant designs to serve an ever-diversifying array of customers and purposes continually being developed and introduced.[3]

In these and other ways, frontline innovators at Fiskars are given the opportunities and resources they need to create a steady stream of innovative concepts. But midlevel coaches and senior leaders also have roles to play in the creation process.

Midlevel coaches, for example, are the first ones to give the employees they supervise permission to innovate. They must also provide these employees with the tools and resources needed to generate innovative ideas, as well as the freedom to devote time and energy to innovation. At Fiskars, the understanding that this is an important part of the middle management role is deeply rooted. "We've embraced the concept of continuous improvement," Enckell told me, "which means that our frontline people are encouraged to think every day about how our products and services can be made better. It's not just about inventing new products or new product lines. It's about small changes that accumulate over time, generating big improvements in the value we create for customers."

Senior leaders at Fiskars also support and guide the overall creation process through the strategic and managerial actions they take. For example, they organize companywide activities designed to encourage and incentivize innovation. These include Idea Days, during which outside companies that partner with Fiskars (such as retailers and suppliers) are invited to work with Fiskars' experts on brainstorming innovations that can produce value for everyone involved.

Senior leaders are also responsible for identifying the most promising areas of future growth for Fiskars based on their understanding of the global market, competitive pressures, demographic trends, technological developments, and other factors. These ideas are formally defined and updated annually in a document known as the Five-Year Innovation Master Plan, which designates specific areas of focus that the senior leaders ask the middle managers and frontline employees to emphasize in their innovative work. Senior leaders also define the standards of excellence, value-creation, and profitability by which potential innovations are judged.

There's a level of creative tension that's inherent in this process of target- and standard-setting. Kari Kauniskangas, then CEO of Fiskars, summed up his approach to the challenge this way: "It's important for me to make sure our people have the desire, will, and freedom to find better ways of doing business. In search of new ideas, we have to give them permission to go crazy! But we also have to create boxes that define their focus and challenge people to innovate in the areas of greatest need."

Making this balancing act work smoothly is a leadership challenge. It helps that Fiskars is a relatively small company (currently about 7,000 employees). "I know almost everyone at Fiskars," Pepe says. "That makes it easy to sustain an atmosphere of trust and cooperation." And Christian Bachler, whose roots are Austrian, observes that Fiskars' relatively flat hierarchy leads to a democratic corporate culture that seems "very Finnish." "Anyone feels free to share their views," Bachler says, "and even to challenge anyone else. It's clear that everybody can make a difference at Fiskars, and everyone feels empowered to do so."

The integration process at Fiskars is largely driven by midlevel coaches. For example, middle managers at Fiskars organize and manage the system whereby new ideas are turned into concrete projects for development and possible implementation. When a promising concept surfaces, middle management chooses one frontline worker to capture its core attributes in the form of a project template. This template is used to guide the stage-gate process by which the concept is gradually developed and refined, which may include the creation of a simple prototype and its testing by potential customers in a workshop at Fiskars or an outside facility, such as a university lab. If the concept continues to appear promising after these tests are completed, it becomes the formal "property" of an appropriate business unit. The midlevel management team that runs this unit is then responsible for integrating the new idea into everyday business operations as part of Fiskars' execution engine, helping to generate economic value for the company as well as for its customers and its business partners.

The process for developing and implementing innovative ideas is itself continually being refined and improved at Fiskars, largely through the efforts of midlevel managers. For example, Jari Ikaheimonen, business manager for Fiskars' Plant Care business department, told me about how he has worked to make the process of evaluating innovative ideas both simpler and more accurate. Having participated in a similar exercise at a previous company, he recommended that Fiskars adopt a tool known as the Quality Function Deployment (QFD) matrix, which helps team members define specific data they can use to zero in on the product and service characteristics that customers value most. "The result has been an improvement in the quality of our decisions," Ikaheimonen says. "Our sales forecasts for new products are now more accurate, which makes the overall innovation process less risky." Most recently, a new incubator group has been established that is responsible for evaluating and selecting proposals for brand-new business units. Any employee can submit a proposal to this group.

Of course, integration also engages the efforts of frontline innovators and senior leaders. Frontline workers support integration when they work on the project development and testing process, as well as when they participate in interdepartmental and multidisciplinary teams and meetings that spread innovating ideas and activities throughout the company. And senior leaders shape the overall integration process through the corporate governance decisions they make—for example, in designing and overseeing the project development system, and in crafting employee evaluation and compensation programs that incentivize innovating.

Finally, the reframing process is driven, above all, by the company's senior leaders. The C-suite executives in an organization are responsible for the long-term strategic thinking that defines the future of the business—which, in turn, shapes the nature of innovation at the company and the way employees imagine and envision their work. This is a task that Fiskars CEO Kari Kauniskangas was deeply engaged in when I visited the company's headquarters. (He has since retired from the position; as of 2021, Nathalie Ahlström holds the role of Fiskars CEO.)

When I met with Kauniskangas, he listed for me some of the most urgent reframing questions he and his team were grappling with. They included: How are Fiskars' customers and their preferences changing? How are the distribution channels we use for our products evolving? What are the implications of these changes for the nature of the work we do? Twenty years from now, will Fiskars continue to sell products in stores, or will our business model have completely changed? Will we be providing access to products through some kind of subscription model rather than through traditional purchasing methods? Will we use 3D printing or other forms of additive manufacturing to localize the design and production of tools? Will our business become primarily a matter of developing and selling intellectual property?

In short, the CEO and C-suite team are continually asking, What kind of company does Fiskars need to become to continue to win in the future? This is the kind of ultimate reframing question that needs to guide the innovative thinking of today's organizations.

Guided by the reframing thinking that takes place at the highest levels of the company, midlevel coaches and frontline innovators at Fiskars are engaging in similar kinds of open-ended discovery. They play a major role in ensuring that a culture of innovating permeates the organization at all levels. In this way, the commitment to innovation that the senior leaders embrace can be turned into concrete actions that produce measurable, valuable results both for Fiskars and for all the company's stakeholders.

During one of my visits to Fiskars, business manager Jari Ikaheimonen made a comment that helped me see how the spirit of reframing has impacted his work at the middle-manager level. "Fiskars is an old, well-established company with a great tradition that we all appreciate," he said. "But today it has also become a fast-growing organization filled with young people who don't feel limited by that tradition. We honor the past, but we don't feel as though we have to own it or defend it. We have permission to innovate in ways that will ensure that Fiskars remains creative and relevant to generations to come."

And Christian Bachler, at that time another midlevel manager in charge of Fiskars' kitchen tools business, captured the same reframing spirit even more succinctly. "Fiskars," he said with a smile, "is a 370-year-old startup."[4]

Reframing with a Global Mindset

In 2019, responding to changes in the world economy, in customer preferences, and in environmental pressures, Fiskars embarked on a particularly ambitious innovating program. Known as Vintage Service, this initiative is about making Fiskars a pioneer in what sustainability experts call *the circular economy,* in which waste is eliminated through the continuous reuse and recycling of all resources and materials. In 2016, Finland became the first country in the world to publish a road map for achieving the circular economy. As one of Finland's leading corporations, Fiskars has been eager to play its part.

Some of the ways Fiskars is working to reduce waste and improve the sustainability of its manufacturing and marketing efforts are similar to those employed by other companies. For example, during 2019, the Gerber brand of specialized knives and other tools, owned by Fiskars, redesigned its packaging and shipping practices to reduce the volume of plastic used and substitute fully recyclable and renewable materials. Similarly, the Iittala factory in Finland has introduced a special version of its popular Raami tumbler made entirely from reused waste glass—one of the first such industrial products in the world. And between 2017 and 2019, the total amount of material sent to landfills by Fiskars companies fell by 61 percent, with further reductions expected to follow.

However, beyond all these laudable efforts, Fiskars is also developing an innovative business model designed particularly to shift the company in the direction of the circular economy. This is the idea that underlies the Vintage Service project. In the words of Nora Haatainen, business director of Vintage Service, "Our aim is to reuse or recycle all the waste generated within our manufacturing facilities and send no waste to landfills."[5]

Customers participate in Vintage Service by selling used glass and ceramic tableware made by the Iittala and Arabia brands back to the company. Fiskars then resells the products to other customers. Items that can't be resold because they are broken will be accepted for recycling in other forms—for example, ceramics are ground into power that is used in brick production, while glass items are transformed into building insulation.

In addition to generating environmental benefits, the Vintage Service system is creating new forms of value for loyal Fiskars customers. Lotta Eskolin is service manager for the Vintage program. "The selection of Vintage items in each store changes every day," she says, "and we've seen gems from decades past and recent years alike. Our customers find missing parts of their collections or complement their table setting with items like sugar bowls or sauce boats. Timeless, thoughtful design lasts for years, and can be passed from one generation to the next."[6]

Customers have embraced the Vintage Service system enthusiastically. Within a few months of its launch, Fiskars estimated that Vintage Service had already reduced waste of natural resources by more than 133 tons, while also reducing carbon emissions by more than 45 tons. By October 2020, Vintage Service had been introduced at every Iittala and Arabia retail store in Finland; expansion into stores in Sweden was about to begin; and Fiskars had broadened the program to include acceptance of *all* manufacturers' brands of tableware for recycling (though not for resale).

Vintage Service is a great illustration of how large-scale reframing concepts can become the basis of practical innovations for frontline employees and midlevel managers to design and implement. The circular economy is an idea that is much bigger than Fiskars or even the Finnish national economy. It's an attempt to redefine how human beings interact with their environment in order to make our connection with the planet more healthy and sustainable.

In a world confronted by multiple crises, from climate change and global pandemics to economic inequality and social injustice, innovative thinking and action at this level is becoming increasingly important. Companies like Fiskars, where all the innovative processes are at work at every level of the organization, are leading the way.

●—●—●

In this chapter, we've seen how the three processes of innovating can permeate your entire organization, thereby maximizing the power and value of the innovative capability of your people. In the next three chapters, we'll look even more closely at each of these levels of the organization and discuss in more detail the roles played by workers at each level in the overall work of innovating.

KEY TAKEAWAYS FROM CHAPTER 5

- All three processes of innovating—creation, integration, and reframing—should take place *in every part of your organization,* including at all three levels: frontline innovators, midlevel coaches, and senior leaders.
- *Creation is often driven largely by frontline innovators,* who have hands-on connections with your daily work processes and continual exposure to the needs and interests of customers as well as the insights provided by noncustomers.
- *Integration is typically driven mainly by midlevel coaches,* who design and implement the processes by which innovative ideas are evaluated, developed, and executed; they also facilitate connections among innovators in different departments of the organization.
- *Reframing is usually driven by senior leaders,* whose work includes continually analyzing trends in the marketplace that may call for changes in the organization's strategic thinking—and perhaps even a reimagining of the company's fundamental identity, purpose, and goals.

PART THREE

THE THREE KEY ROLES IN INNOVATING

6

HANDS-ON CREATIVITY

HOW TO INSPIRE AND EMPOWER YOUR COMPANY'S FRONTLINE INNOVATORS

Running a hotel is one of the most grueling jobs you can imagine. Every day, there are thousands of small, essential tasks that must be done correctly, from serving the breakfast toast while it's still hot to fixing a balky Stairmaster in the fitness center to shuttling a departing guest to the airport on time. Botch one task, and you may have lost a customer forever. Under daily, detail-oriented pressure like this, it's tough for hotel managers to generate big, innovative ideas for the future of their industry—which is why most hotel chains today offer me-too products and services.

How, then, did the giant Starwood organization—operators of 850 hotels in 95 countries under brand names that include Sheraton, Westin, W, and St Regis—inspire its managers to generate no fewer than 1,700 innovative ideas . . . all in a single day?

Perhaps we can attribute it on the magic of Paris.

Robyn Pratt, then vice president for Six Sigma and operational innovation at Starwood, Europe, Africa, and the Middle East, organized the day during a conference in Paris attended by the company's managers from Pratt's whole region. Asked to find a way to jump-start fresh thinking about the future of Starwood, Pratt organized the 700 attendees into 64 teams and assigned each team one of eight words reflecting the company's core values: beauty, trust, thoughtfulness, luxury, individuality, inspiration, style, approachability. Then she sent the teams out to roam the streets of Paris with notebooks and cameras, challenging them to find images, experiences, and insights that embodied those words.

Three hours later, the 700 managers came back with an amazing wealth of stories and ideas. Street scenes, the famous parks and fountains of the city, intimate glimpses of Parisian family life, the elaborate awnings over the windows at Maxim's restaurant, a young couple kissing on the Metro—all were fodder for fresh insights into the nature and meaning of Starwood's hospitality brands. The 1,700 ideas that poured out were captured and sorted for possible use in improving the hotel's day-to-day operations. Some turned into minor improvements to existing projects, others into clever new advertising or promotional concepts, and still others grew into major strategic initiatives that Starwood adopted globally—like FamTASTIC, a marketing approach that develops special family packages based on research into what kids, not their parents, want from a hotel.

None of the 700 managers who took part in this exercise was a specialist in innovation. But once the managers were taken out of their daily work routine, given permission to innovate, and taught a few simple mind-expanding tools, they produced a flood of new ideas—many with the potential to create huge new value for Starwood. Afterward, one participant commented, "I didn't know I was a creative type, but now I think I can do it."[1]

Why Frontline Innovators Play a Crucial Role in the Process of Creation

As I've explained, one of the foundational processes of innovating is *creation*—the generation of ideas for new products, services, process improvements, or other innovations that may benefit the organization as well as its various stakeholders. Most often, the crucial actors in the creation process are *frontline innovators*. These could include assembly-line workers and foremen in a factory, actuaries and sales agents in an insurance company, and nurses and physicians in a hospital. In the case of Starwood, they were frontline managers from throughout the hotel chain— people who spent most of their days interacting with guests.

When these frontline workers operate within the execution engine, they focus on doing their assigned tasks as well as possible—as they should. But when they enter the innovating engine—as all employees should do from time to time—a shift in mental gears is required. While inside the innovating engine, their minds and actions should be totally focused on looking for new value-creating business ideas.

The potential of frontline workers to generate such ideas is enormous. Frontline innovators are the employees who directly face customers (and often noncustomers, too) in the greatest numbers and with the greatest frequency. Thus, they have the most numerous opportunities to learn from customers about their unmet needs, unspoken desires, and unsolved problems— each of which represents a possible opportunity for innovation by the organization.

In addition to serving customers, frontline innovators are also directly engaged in most of the other processes that are central to the organization's business model. Frontline workers are personally involved in making products, delivering services, managing financial transactions, designing apps and webpages, handling human resource functions, and carrying out all the other activities that, through their cumulative impact, lead to success or failure for the company. No wonder frontline workers are in the best possible position to generate ideas about how to make those activities work better.

Unfortunately, in many organizations, frontline workers don't get the respect they deserve. Many frontline jobs are entry-level positions that end up being filled by employees with little or no experience and few specialized skills. The pay, prestige, and power associated with these jobs are often minimal. And when specific frontline employees stand out from their peers because of their unusual talent, efficiency, and creativity, they usually get promoted into the managerial ranks—which means they stop being frontline workers.

The result is a paradoxical one. In many organizations, the higher employees rise in the business hierarchy, the less hands-on, face-to-face contact they have with customers and with the work processes that actually produce revenues and profits for the company. As they move up the ladder to become midlevel managers, and, in some cases, senior executives, they gain increasing power to innovate—yet, at the same time, they lose the continual first-hand access to customers and processes that helps to generate innovative ideas.

Fortunately, there's a way to resolve this paradox. Organizations that want to embed innovating in their DNA must recognize the crucial role that frontline innovators play. These organizations need to develop ways to incentivize frontline workers to devote time and energy to developing and sharing innovative ideas. They also need to create systems that surface those ideas, identify the best ones, and turn them into practical realities. Frontline employees can benefit enormously from the creative opportunities such systems provide—and the companies they work for can benefit even more.

How a Hospitality Giant Uses Customer Intimacy to Fuel Innovation—and Vice Versa

Shortly after the Paris adventure I described at the start of this chapter, the Starwood organization was acquired by Marriott International. The new combination created the world's largest hotel company. Embracing 30 different hotel brands that operate some 6,700 individual hotels in 130 countries around the world, the Marriott organization faces the challenge of efficiently running a vast operation while staying closely in touch with the needs, wishes, and preferences of millions of individual customers. Empowering and listening to frontline employees is crucial to carrying out this complex balancing act between execution and innovating—and one of the reasons Marriott chose to acquire Starwood seems to have been the company's widely recognized talent for innovation.

In recent years, one important arena for innovation in the hospitality industry has been social media. This is a challenge that businesses in practically every industry have been dealing with. Social media platforms from Facebook and Twitter to Instagram and WhatsApp have made it easy for individuals to broadcast their experiences, feelings, and opinions about companies to thousands or even millions of people around the world. Hospitality businesses must also pay attention to specialized platforms like TripAdvisor, Expedia, and Kayak, which wield a huge influence over the travel decisions made by countless customers.

Starwood was a pioneer among hospitality companies in tapping social media as a source of innovative ideas. For example, Starwood was one of the first companies in any industry to empower team members in its customer service centers to proactively monitor comments about their business appearing on social media sites. These frontline employees were also empowered to periodically "surprise and delight" individual customers by offering them benefits and gifts tailored to their interests as expressed online. Starwood also pioneered such creative social media tactics as displaying hotel menus in photo layouts on Instagram, which proved to be a uniquely effective method for reaching millennial and Gen X travelers. Starwood was also one of the first companies to jump on the bandwagon when Snapchat took off, which enabled the hotel chain to engage four million additional customers within just a few months.[2] All of these examples show how Starwood led the way in using social media as a tool for understanding and responding to the needs of customers—a classic illustration of the unique role that frontline innovators are positioned to play.

Starwood also excelled at learning from customers using traditional, low-tech tools. Mark Vondrasek, formerly the head of Starwood's customer loyalty program and currently chief commercial officer at Hyatt Hotels, described how the company created its Ambassador program to provide a channel for making customer needs and preferences into sources of innovative thinking. The Starwood Ambassadors were a special cadre of frontline employees trained to serve as the single point of contact for individual travelers. Through repeated contact, the Ambassadors got to know a variety of Starwood customers intimately—globe-trotting business travelers, families with small children, young adults backpacking on a budget—thereby learning a lot about what these customers really needed and wanted.

To take full advantage of the insights these frontline workers were developing, Starwood convened twice-a-month meetings that gave the Ambassadors an opportunity to report on their observations and suggest innovative ideas. Starwood also modified its human resources policies to incentivize innovating by these frontline workers. Vondrasek explains:

> One thing we had struggled with before was the "pyramid effect": if you were talented on the [customer service] phones and wanted to progress, you pretty much had to become your supervisor. Now, we have new opportunities for these employees. We've

even created paths from the Ambassador program to sales roles in our various properties—something that didn't exist five years ago. As a result of all this, turnover in our contact centers went down and employee satisfaction went up.[3]

Here's one example of the way the Ambassador program systematized frontline innovation at Starwood. The hotel chain developed a new benefit for its frequent guests called YOUR24. It came about as a result of complaints from international travelers who often arrived from overseas early in the morning, having taken red-eye flights from Europe or Asia. Exhausted, they were frustrated by having to wait until the mandated 3 p.m. check-in time before they could get access to their hotel rooms. Created in response to suggestions by the Ambassador team, YOUR24 was one of the first hotel programs to let guests choose their own check-in time—a differentiating feature that enabled Starwood to attract and retain the loyalty of more international travelers than rival hotel chains.

Since acquiring Starwood, Marriott has continued to develop the same kinds of frontline-driven innovations. In 2019, it launched the Marriott Bonvoy app, which facilitates a host of activities for on-the-go travelers, from remote check-in and mobile key delivery to the use of chatbots to receive instant responses to simple questions. Marriott also became the first major hotel chain to offer a customized version of Alexa, the voice-activated personal assistant created by Amazon. Alexa for Hospitality serves as a "virtual concierge" for Marriott guests, making it easy for them to request services from extra towels to local restaurant recommendations.[4]

Notice two crucial features that link all these innovations from Starwood and Marriott—the pro-active use of social media, the Ambassador program, the Bonvoy app. First, these innovations all originated in response to unmet customer needs that were recognized and highlighted by frontline employees. Second, in varying ways, they all help to bring frontline innovators and customers into even closer connection, creating opportunities to provide better, more responsive services that make Marriott guests even more loyal.

For this hotel giant, the ideas produced by frontline innovators reflect an unusually high degree of customer intimacy—and at the same time, they also help to increase that intimacy for the future. Thus, the way Marriott empowers and incentivizes its frontline innovators creates a virtuous cycle that benefits both the hotel chain and the millions of travelers around the world whom it serves.

Valve: Making *Everyone* in the Business a Frontline Innovator

In the quest for innovation, big, established companies like Marriott are often seen as being at a disadvantage when compared with smaller, newer businesses. There are a number of reasons why this might be so. Startup companies generally have less bureaucracy than older ones; they've had less time to develop rules, regulations, and policies that define and limit what employees can do, which can discourage the outside-of-the-box thinking that's necessary for innovation to occur. Smaller companies are usually more aggressive about pursuing growth opportunities; because their revenue bases and profit margins are smaller, they are hungry to find ways of attracting new customers, and therefore more willing to take chances on new business concepts than their larger, more comfortable rivals. And smaller, newer companies lack the histories of success that older businesses boast, which means they are less likely to be tempted to "rest on their laurels" and assume that the same strategies and philosophies that brought them this far will suffice to carry them successfully into the future.

All of these well-known factors surely play a role in explaining why big, long-established companies often struggle to innovate, and must make special efforts to keep their innovating engines humming. But one of the less widely recognized reasons that small startup companies are often more innovative than large, established firms is that they have a higher percentage of frontline employees. Newer firms generally offer fewer products or services and have fewer workers, simpler administrative structures, and few or no layers of hierarchical decision makers. As a result, practically everyone works directly with customers. The high percentage of frontline workers means innovation has a chance to pop up almost everywhere—and it often does.

A handful of companies have sought to maintain this spirit even after years of growth. They seek to avoid becoming hierarchical and bureaucratic, instead encouraging employees to stay in close contact with customers and to make independent decisions about how they spend their time. These companies also try to minimize the need for approvals from managers, and to treat all team members as more or less equal in status and power.

In effect, these companies try to inspire *everyone* in the company to behave like frontline employees. They hope in this way to inspire levels of innovation and creativity that most companies can only dream about.

Of course, there are good reasons why most companies develop managerial hierarchies and bureaucratic systems as they grow. Sheer size and complexity makes it hard for businesses to operate their execution engines successfully without such organizational tools. Therefore, relatively few large companies have managed to operate according to the low-hierarchy, maximal freedom model. However, the few that have succeeded in doing so offer some important lessons that other companies should consider in managing their innovating engines.

One large business that has striven to remain relatively nonhierarchical and nonbureaucratic is W. L. Gore, the materials innovation company discussed in Chapters 2 and 3. Though Gore is not completely free of managerial layers and bureaucratic controls, it provides frontline employees with a greater degree of freedom than most corporations, including the freedom to explore a diverse range of customer needs and develop innovative projects up to a point in pursuit of their own interests. As we've seen, Gore has successfully built a substantial business using this unusual managerial model.

An industry in which the low-hierarchy model is relatively common is software development. There's a good reason for this. Most employees in a software development firm spend their time mainly on creative work, which is not true of companies in most industries. In effect, the typical proportional relationship between the execution engine and the innovating engine is upended. At most companies, the execution engine is much larger than the innovating engine; in the world of software development, the reverse is true. Thus, organizing the entire business using a management model that encourages creativity and innovation, even at the expense of other values such as efficiency and consistency, may make good sense.

A software firm known for its nonhierarchical structure is Menlo Associates, an Ann Arbor, Michigan–based company that specializes in custom business software and consulting services. Rather than creating conventional work teams led by a manager, Menlo Associates pairs up developers who work on projects together, switching partners periodically to keep the teams fresh and their creative juices flowing. The company likes to describe itself as being "in the business of joy," and the company's cofounder, Richard Sheridan, described its innovative methods in a 2015 book titled *Joy, Inc.*[5]

Another example is GitHub, which provides internet hosting services and systems for managing distributed software development. Founded in 2008, the company originally designed its structure to be one in which "everyone is a manager" and in which every employee had the freedom to choose the projects he or she worked on. GitHub operated in this fashion quite successfully for several years. However, in 2014, having grown significantly and encountered some of the organizational challenges that most expanding businesses face, it installed a middle management layer. Four years later, GitHub was purchased by Microsoft, and it is now run as a more-or-less conventional division of that technology giant.

Perhaps the most famous nonhierarchical software company is Valve Corporation, a Bellevue, Washington–based video game designer. Founded in 1996 by two refugees from Microsoft, Valve as of 2021 has over 300 employees and, while privately held, has an estimated value well over $3 billion. Valve's super-popular games, including *Half-Life* and *Counter-Strike,* have won dozens of game-of-the-year awards, and its online gaming portal Steam is the world's most popular. For some 15 years, Valve was arguably the most successful video game development company in the world, until—as you'll see—its business model dramatically shifted.

During its decade and a half at the top of the video game business, what made Valve particularly unusual was the fact that it was virtually devoid of managerial layers. No one at Valve was considered anyone's "boss." (The closest thing was company founder Gabe Newell, who had the power to fire someone when he deemed it necessary.) Workers at Valve chose the projects they wanted to work on or launched their own. Self-selected, multidisciplinary teams called "cabals" formed organically around interesting topics, from which products often emerged. And as soon as any group of three or more employees believed a new product was ready for the marketplace, they were empowered to ship it, with no need for approval by anyone else.

One employee's blog post summarized well the thinking behind Valve's antihierarchical philosophy. The post began by making the point that, in the world of video games, innovation is the single most important source of business value. It then continued:

If most of the value is now in the initial creative act, there's little benefit to traditional hierarchical organization that's designed to deliver the same thing over and over, making only incremental changes over time. What matters is being first and bootstrapping your product into a positive feedback spiral with a constant stream of creative innovation. Hierarchical management doesn't help with that, because it bottlenecks innovation through the people at the top of the hierarchy, and there's no reason to expect that those people would be particularly creative about coming up with new products that are dramatically different from existing ones—quite the opposite, in fact. So Valve was designed as a company that would attract the sort of people capable of taking the initial creative step, leave them free to do creative work, and make them want to stay. Consequently, Valve has no formal management or hierarchy at all.[6]

As this blog post explained, Valve's nonhierarchical management structure was designed specifically to make frontline innovating as fast and easy as possible. In the words of one observer, Valve believed that "each employee is capable of producing your company's disruptive technology or service"—so why not give every employee the freedom, the flexibility, and the tools to do just that?[7]

This management system—which perhaps should be called a "nonsystem"—worked brilliantly for Valve. But the company itself acknowledged that its management nonsystem wouldn't work everywhere. Among other things, a nonhierarchical structure requires employees who are very smart, self-motivated, team-oriented, and ultra-flexible. The *Valve Handbook for New Employees*, which is available online, is quite frank about the fact that the company's philosophy has both strengths and weaknesses. It contains a section headed "What Is Valve *Not* Good

At?" that lists six things the company has struggled to do, including "Helping people find their way," "Mentoring people," and "Disseminating information internally."[8] This degree of honesty is admirable. It also reflects some of the challenges that generally arise when a company tries to manage without clear, organized structures, team-management protocols, decision-making processes, and communications systems.

As I've said, Valve operated as a nonhierarchical game developer with enormous success for some 15 years. More recently, however, the company's business model has changed. The seeds of this shift were planted back in 2003 with the company's launch of Steam, an online storefront for the games produced by Valve. Soon the company decided to offer games produced by other developers on Steam. The platform proved to be so popular that the value of Steam exploded to the point where it dwarfed the value produced by Valve's own games. Today, Steam is the world's dominant distributor of video games, offering more than 34,000 games that are available in 28 languages and reach over 95 million monthly users. Steam's revenues for 2017 (the last year for which data are available from this privately held company) exceeded $4.3 billion.

The rise of the Steam platform has ended up eclipsing the company's original purpose. While Steam has come to dominate the gaming marketplace, Valve's creativity as a game developer has largely stalled. The company continued to release popular games through the mid-2010s, but the product flow gradually diminished, and today Valve produces just a handful of new games each year. Many of the top-flight game developers who were once thrilled to work at Valve have departed.

Observers offer varying explanations for this change. Some concluded that Valve's nonhierarchical management structure simply stopped working. Others, however, blame the decline in game-design creativity on the overwhelming success of Steam. "There is clearly a lot more money in being an Amazon-style distribution platform than in developing games," one journalist concluded.[9]

Stories like those of Menlo Associates, GitHub, and Valve illustrate how difficult it is to maintain a nonhierarchical management structure for long. Yet they also suggest that, while such a structure is in place, the freedom it provides to frontline innovators can produce tremendous benefits both for companies and their stakeholders.

Hierarchy, Rules, and Creativity: Lessons for Running a Great Innovating Engine

When we look at companies that do an especially good job of empowering their frontline innovators, some managerial patterns seem clear. In particular, it's important for companies to strive to run their innovating engines with as much freedom and flexibility as possible—even while their execution engines may need traditional hierarchies and rules in order to carry out the daily functions of the business with as much efficiency and consistency as possible.

This doesn't necessarily mean that your innovating engine should be devoid of hierarchies and rules. But companies can benefit from striving to minimize the degree to which they allow such administrative growths to creep in, since they tend to limit the creativity that frontline innovators need. For example, they can seek to emulate Netflix, a big, successful business that prides itself on making an effort to keep rules and hierarchies to a minimum—not to the extreme extent that Valve did, but far more than most companies of their size have managed to do.

The story of the Netflix system is told by company founder Reed Hastings and INSEAD professor Erin Meyer in their book *No Rules Rules*.[10] Hastings recounts how he learned to hate stifling hierarchies and rigid rules during his previous corporate jobs. Thus, when he founded Netflix and began building it into a successful movie distributor, he vowed that he would keep the company's bureaucratic structure as simple and unobtrusive as possible. Among the unusual results: the company is famous for having no rules controlling the number of vacation days employees can take, the sums they can spend on corporate travel, even the amounts they can invest in business initiatives. Netflix's Culture Deck, a famous collection of slides that summarizes the company's business philosophy, encourages employees to operate according to such maxims as "Lead with context, not control," and "Don't seek to please your boss." Thus, the entirety of Netflix—not just its innovating engine—is managed with as much freedom from rules and regulations as possible.

People who join Netflix from traditionally run companies are often shocked by the level of freedom they enjoy. Some can't handle it: every year, a few newcomers quit because they don't feel comfortable making business decisions without having a boss who must review and approve their choices. And a tiny handful abuse the system: *No Rules Rules* tells the story of one Netflix employee who had to be fired after it was discovered that he'd arranged to be reimbursed for over $100,000 worth of lavish vacations over three years.

Founder Reed Hastings acknowledges that there are necessary limits to the principle of allowing employees to make decisions on their own. In industries outside of the world of entertainment, such a model may not be workable. Hastings observes that "high-volume, low-error" businesses in which errors can affect critical matters like safety—pharmaceutical manufacturing, for example—may require traditional methods of control. Netflix itself enforces limiting rules in areas "where error prevention is clearly more important than innovation," such as financial reporting and customer data privacy. The execution engine, in other words, is generally *not* a place where absolute freedom from rules and processes is desirable.

What's more, even when it comes to innovation, Netflix is not completely without rules and processes. For example, one of the company's core innovation principles is to require employees to "farm for dissent" before launching any new initiative—that is, to proactively seek feedback from colleagues, especially contrary opinions that might highlight weaknesses that need to be eliminated. Thus, Netflix's innovating engine does involve rules and procedures, though these are kept as minimal as possible.

Nonetheless, for a large company (with revenues of over $1.8 billion as of 2019), Netflix is unusually free of rules and hierarchical practices that limit the freedom of frontline employees to innovate. And the evidence shows that Netflix has been extremely successful—and also highly innovative. Since going public in 2002, its stock price has risen from $1 per share to more than $500 (as of January 2021). It has achieved this sustained success by successfully navigating changes in an entertainment industry undergoing a series of dramatic technological and market shifts that have staggered many of its competitors. Finally, most employees like the opportunities to innovate that the Netflix system provides: in a 2018 survey, tech workers rated Netflix as the #1 company they'd like to work for. Being able to attract top talent in this way is a big competitive advantage for Netflix.

Of course, it's important to note that, like Valve and the other software development companies we looked at earlier, Netflix is centered on innovating to an unusual degree. Most of the company's employees spend most of their time purely on creative work, such as developing new films and television programs for distribution to Netflix's millions of subscribers. This is not true of companies in most industries. Because the entire company is focused almost exclusively on innovating, it can be organized in a way that encourages maximum individual freedom and creativity.

For this reason, I think it makes sense for most business leaders to look at the management structures of Valve and Netflix as potential models for their companies' innovating engines—but not necessarily for their execution engines. In many industries, you're likely to find that you need to maintain a traditional, hierarchical structure for your execution engine while encouraging employees to interact and operate in a much more unstructured, free-flowing fashion while working in the parallel innovating engine.

I'd also suggest that Valve's aspiration to operate completely without bosses is probably a bridge too far for most companies. Perhaps the innovation lesson most businesses can take from these company stories is not "*Eliminate* hierarchy in your innovating engine" but rather "Keep hierarchy *to a minimum* in your innovating engine, thereby empowering and incentivizing the innovative instincts of your frontline workers." It's a less ambitious, less revolutionary approach than the one Valve embraced—but one that can help keep your innovating engine humming even as your company grows.

KEY TAKEAWAYS FROM CHAPTER 6

- While employees throughout the organization should participate in all three processes of innovating, there is *a special role to be played* by those in each of the three main organizational levels.
- *Frontline employees are especially important in the creation process* because they usually interact most frequently and directly with customers (and noncustomers) of all kinds, as well as with the other important processes and activities of the company.
- Frontline employees should be encouraged, empowered, and incentivized to pay special attention to the needs, desires, and unsolved problems of customers, each of which should be treated as a potential opportunity for innovation.
- In most companies, the execution engine needs to be managed using traditional organizational tools that include a leadership hierarchy as well as rules, systems, and approval processes.
- However, the innovating engine can often benefit by *keeping hierarchical practices and rules to a minimum.* The more freedom your frontline innovators have to be creative, the better your innovating engine will run.

7

COACHING INNOVATION

HOW MIDLEVEL MANAGERS NURTURE THE SYSTEMS THAT MAKE INNOVATING POSSIBLE

Several years ago, I had the opportunity to train a group of executives from Allianz, the German financial giant, in innovation techniques at the Allianz Management Institute in Kempfenhausen, near Munich. It came at the request of Jan Carendi, an Argentina-born executive who was then a member of the board of Allianz. He had visited me at INSEAD's campus in the suburbs of Paris to learn more about how to apply Blue Ocean Strategy to the process of innovating—a topic of special interest, because Allianz was then in the midst of creating a systematic approach to generating and implementing innovative ideas throughout its businesses. Carendi and

I ended up spending almost an entire day walking in the forest of Fontainebleau and discussing the philosophy of innovation.

At a certain point in our conversation, Carendi offered an observation that I remember to this day, and which I often quote when people ask me to describe what is necessary to stimulate innovating. "To innovate," Carendi said, "people need to feel *able, capable,* and *motivated.*" I think that simple sentence suggests very well three of the most important elements an organization's leaders must provide if they expect their people to participate in innovating: they must give them permission to innovate (that is, letting them feel "able"); they must give them the skills, support, and tools they need to innovate (helping them to be "capable"); and they must nurture in them the desire to innovate (making them feel "motivated").

Hoping to provide the Allianz team with these three essential ingredients for innovation, Carendi asked me to share my innovating approach with a group of about 30 company leaders. This project was a fascinating challenge for me. After all, the world of insurance in which Allianz competes is not generally regarded as a hotbed of innovation. Insurance is a mature industry that employs business models developed more than a century ago; it pursues profitability through conservative strategies for avoiding financial risk and minimizing the impact of unpredictable fluctuations in economic variables such as interest rates and currency values. It was quite a departure from the norm to have one of the world's leading insurance companies invite a specialist in innovation to speak to its middle management team about how to inspire creative thinking among its frontline employees.

So I was a bit surprised, but also delighted, when I found that the Allianz executives were fascinated by my presentation and eager to try applying the principles of innovating to their own operations. Fired with enthusiasm, they invited me to observe and offer guidance as they worked on building an innovating engine for Allianz. Dr. Werner Zedelius, another member of the Allianz board, was the sponsor of this global innovating project.

I ended up training more than 100 additional Allianz executives over a series of programs.

The midlevel managers conducted training sessions in which they shared the basic principles of innovating with the frontline workers who reported to them. They also created an internal information system designed to let any employee from an Allianz division generate and share innovating ideas. The ideas were then funneled to a corporate-level committee whose job was to select projects to be acted upon. The goal was to create a process by which innovative concepts could be turned into practical realities, both improving the operations of Allianz and providing benefits to the company's stakeholders, from customers to employees.

It was a well-crafted system, but it had one flaw. Within three months, it became overloaded with ideas from hundreds of Allianz workers. Swamped with ideas, the committee was unable to respond in a timely fashion—and when workers found that their suggestions went unanswered for weeks or even months, the rate of submissions plummeted.

In some companies, the leadership might have been so discouraged that the whole concept of creating an innovation information system might simply have been abandoned. To its credit, Allianz recognized the fact that the problem was actually an amazing opportunity—a reflection of the pent-up creativity of the company's employees, who had been sitting on innovative ideas for years. Rather than giving up, Allianz devised a simple solution. In each division of the company, a local innovation coordinator was appointed and given the mandate to provide preliminary feedback on every concept within 15 days of its submission. The flow of creative ideas quickly resumed.

The Allianz story illustrates a fundamental truth about innovating: Generating a huge number of promising ideas is just the first step in the process. Equally important is a system that will winnow the ideas, channel them in the best directions, develop them into viable business concepts, provide them with investment money, connect them to the key people in the organization who can contribute to them, and ultimately launch them with the greatest possible odds of success. Creating and maintaining such a system is a crucial job for your company's middle managers.

In this chapter, we'll explore how midlevel coaches can create and sustain the organizational systems that enable frontline innovators to turn their bright ideas into practical realities.

How Midlevel Coaches at Allianz Helped Build a Worldwide System for Innovation

Stimulated in part by the training programs I provided, the leaders of Allianz went on to refine and develop the innovating system they launched so as to make the most of the flood of ideas their frontline employees were generating. The system Allianz devised—itself a great example of innovative thinking—used clear, simple metrics to track the flow of ideas, broken down to the division level, and to turn the entire process into a competitive exercise. Wade Harvey, the local innovation manager for Allianz UK, explained it to me. "We publish an innovation league table on a regular basis that shows the relative performance of each division within our UK operation," Wade said. "No one wants to be seen at the lower end of the scale, so it tends to have a positive side effect in terms of motivating leaders." This system helped keep all of Allianz's employees excited and engaged in the innovating process. Treating innovation as a team sport—and tracking and publicizing the players' statistics, just as football and baseball teams do—proved to be a powerful way to ensure that innovating remains front and center in the minds of the company's employees.

As part of a corporate initiative dubbed Ideas to Success (*i2s*), Allianz went on to expand its innovating program into a decentralized set of projects that spanned the globe.[1] Led by a headquarters team in Munich and with oversight and board support from Dr. Zedelius, a network of 72 local innovation managers in 37 countries took on the jobs of coaching frontline employees in innovating techniques, selecting the best ideas, and steering individual initiatives to successful implementation. These local innovation managers represented Allianz's first attempt to create a cadre of company leaders who could systematize the practice of innovating and support frontline workers in their efforts to generate and develop ideas.

In the years subsequent to my work with them, Allianz went on to become one of the most innovative companies in the insurance industry. The company's innovation system, with outposts in Allianz divisions in countries around the world, has generated thousands of ideas and created tens of millions of dollars in value for its customers and its shareholders. In the process, the system itself has continued to evolve, as Allianz has modified and refined its workings in response to a growing body of evidence regarding what works and what doesn't.

Through the years, the corporation has experimented with a variety of changes to the innovating system. For example, in 2007, just months after *i2s* was launched, Allianz Group announced a Global Innovation Award that gave the creator of an innovative idea a handsome trophy and the opportunity to make a personal presentation to the group CEO. (You might observe that providing this kind of recognition is one way to ensure that people feel "motivated" to innovate, the third crucial ingredient in Carendi's three-part recipe for innovating.)

Other systemic changes were implemented on a country-by-country basis. For example, at Allianz UK, to further encourage a continuing flow of ideas, two new sets of midlevel coaches were created to lead innovation at the local level. One group was labeled "lead champions"; their job was to advocate for innovative ideas during management meetings, making sure that senior decision makers were kept informed about good ideas that were bubbling up from the frontlines. Another group was called "innovation champions"; they worked on coaching and mentoring frontline workers as well as organizing innovation panels and challenges at the local level.[2] (These two groups of midlevel coaches were providing the first two ingredients in the Carendi recipe, helping Allianz employees to be "able" to innovate and "capable" of innovating.)

Over time, the innovation champions played a powerful role in sparking innovation at Allianz. Beginning in 2009, the innovation champions began convening teams of frontline employees to work collaboratively on idea generation, an approach that was shown to generate more and better ideas than solo ideation. They organized and led companywide "idea challenges," in which groups of frontline employees were invited to propose concrete answers to broadly worded questions like, How can we improve the customer experience? The resulting ideas were winnowed by review panels that included both the innovation champions and selected subject-matter experts, who identified specific concepts that could become the basis of practical initiatives.

In addition, the innovation champions served as *connectors,* finding ways to link individuals with good ideas with colleagues throughout the company who had the knowledge, experience, and resources to help develop and implement those ideas. As one manager put it, "We communicate to our staff this message: when you come up with an idea, rather than thinking you should execute it or you can deliver the whole idea completely by yourself, you should form teams and collaborate with other people to get things done."[3] From their in-between level in the company hierarchy—in close touch with frontline employees but also with enough elevation to have visibility into other departments and divisions—midlevel coaches like Allianz's innovation champions are uniquely well positioned to help forge such vital connections.

Allianz's corporatewide system for innovating, built heavily on the contributions of midlevel coaches, enabled company divisions around the world to generate fresh approaches to the insurance business that have produced enhanced value for the company as well as for its customers. An example is one of the world's first digital ecosystems to help protect the lives and property of consumers by using integrated monitoring and communication tools based on the emerging Internet of Things (IoT). Initially launched in Allianz's home territory of Germany, Smart Home + Allianz Assist monitors customers' homes around the clock, detecting dangers such as fire, flood, and burglary; sending help immediately; and even initiating insurance claims to quickly cover the costs of any damage.[4]

Another example is a project by which the 4,300 agents employed by Malaysia's Allianz Life Insurance subsidiary are being "reskilled" to use digital tools that can now get new policies approved in just five minutes rather than the 24 hours usually considered standard. As a result, says the company's CEO, "Allianz is the only insurer who can improve policies over a cup of tea."[5] And yet another example is Allie, an artificial intelligence–powered virtual assistant that serves Allianz customers in Taiwan using natural language processing in fluent Mandarin to answer complex insurance questions and make policy adjustments at any hour of the day or night.[6]

As these examples suggest, like businesses in almost every industry today, insurance companies are under increasing pressure to take full advantage of the innovative possibilities created by an ever-growing range of digital technologies. Allianz was one of the first insurance giants to recognize this emerging reality. The innovation program it launched more than a decade ago, and then expanded around the world through a network of highly trained midlevel coaches, has placed the company at the forefront of this trend—and helped it remain there.

Today, the *i2s* innovation program is no longer a formal part of the Allianz corporate structure. It's not needed, because the culture and process of innovating has become deeply embedded in departments and divisions throughout the company. Continuing support for innovating is provided by a group known as Allianz Consulting. This is a team of about 150 people who are available, on demand, to provide tools, frameworks, and training that Allianz business units can use in managing their innovating projects. The consultants from this group don't think of themselves as "innovation champions"—that role is now filled by team members from the business units, who have become the driving force behind innovating at Allianz.[7]

When Innovating Is Second Nature: How Midlevel Coaches Help Drive Innovation at IBM

Unlike insurance, the world of high technology is a place where innovation is taken for granted. When business leaders want to learn how to make their organizations more innovative, they often turn for inspiration to the famous technology companies created during the dot-com era—companies like Apple, Google, Facebook, Microsoft, and Amazon. It's certainly true that these companies have built huge, successful businesses through breakthrough innovations. But the mystique and glamour surrounding these companies and their famous founders and CEOs can sometimes obscure the lessons about innovation that "ordinary" businesses in traditional industries can apply.

Even within the world of technology, the companies that garner the most headlines for their head-turning innovations aren't necessarily the ones that other business leaders should seek to emulate. For example, if you had to guess which high-tech company receives the most US patents, you might be surprised by the answer. It's not Apple, Google, Facebook, Microsoft, or any other offspring of the dot-com era. Actually, the company registering the largest number of technological innovations in 2020 was IBM, a venerable company. Founded in 1911, it was originally built on information tabulating and computing technologies developed in the 1880s. And the 2020 victory was no fluke—2020 was the twenty-eighth consecutive year that IBM led the patent pack.[8]

Patents, of course, are not the only or even necessarily the best measure of corporate innovation—but they are certainly one metric that can serve as a useful proxy for that elusive quality. IBM has also demonstrated its innovative prowess in many other ways—for example, its ability to repeatedly reframe itself through successive eras of technology, from punch card computers to digital devices and then by becoming a leader in software, computer memory, databases, personal computing, the internet, and, most recently, cognitive computing based in the cloud.[9]

There are many factors that help to explain why IBM continues to be innovative, decade after decade. However, two crucial elements are the cultural dynamics and innovation-driving practices that middle managers at IBM are encouraged to nurture. Kristof Kloeckner, an innovation coach in IBM's Global Technology Services division, lists a number of the key activities he and other midlevel managers have used to foster the company's innovation-centered culture. These activities include:

- ▶ Themed hackathons offering prizes for creative solutions to challenges faced by IBM customers
- ▶ Innovation contests that provide opportunities for junior practitioners to earn such coveted designations as "master inventors" or "agile champions"
- ▶ Rewarding team members not just for patents but also for conference presentations, open-source contributions, and journal articles—all ways of ensuring IBM people remain connected to industrywide thinking[10]

Activities like these, organized and driven by midlevel coaches, are supported by a companywide innovation framework that includes a number of high-profile programs. One is IBM's Emerging Business Opportunity (EBO) system, which originated in 2000 and has evolved, expanded, and morphed in various ways

ever since. It's a process for identifying powerful business opportunities created by important economic and social trends and
then creating cross-company alignment around innovative
strategies for addressing those opportunities. A senior business
leader serves as the sponsor for a particular EBO project, while
active management of the project is delegated to a midlevel manager viewed as having unusual career potential. Specific EBOs
have been developed in a wide range of business areas, from
information-based medicine to new business models for emerging economies. Many have grown into profitable business units
in their own right.[11]

A newer companywide program that helps to support IBM's
midlevel coaches in their role as innovation drivers is the Call for
Code Global Initiative. Launched in 2018, Call for Code is an
open-source project that invites outside contributors—startup
companies, academic experts and students, and corporate partners—to work with IBM tech leaders on problems of global
importance. In 2020, Call for Code focused on two issues
deemed particularly important: the COVID-19 pandemic and
the challenge of achieving racial justice. On a corporate level,
IBM offers significant financial awards of up to $200,000 for the
best innovative solutions that emerge from the program. At the
middle management level, company leaders share tech resources,
tools, and information with outside teams and serve as connectors between IBM employees and people around the world with
potentially powerful innovation ideas.

These programs and others like them have helped to make
IBM's midlevel managers into powerful innovation cheerleaders and coaches. They accelerate the development of frontline
employees, forge connections among innovators both inside and
outside the organization, and keep the stream of bright ideas
flowing swiftly. And because innovating has become so deeply
embedded into IBM's DNA—especially into the thinking and
behavior of the company's numerous midlevel coaches—the
habit of innovating is not just a fad or a short-term focus that

will be dropped when a new CEO is named. Instead, those thousands of lifetime IBM professionals will transmit the innovating gene to rising generations within the company. They make it likely that IBM will retain a spot near the top of the innovation heap for years to come.

How Midlevel Managers Keep the Innovating Engine Humming at Recruit Holdings

IBM has been an innovation leader for more than a century. But plenty of newer companies from a range of industries are using similar leadership techniques to become innovation powerhouses in their own right. One company example that is currently little known in the United States—but poised to change that status in the near future—is a Japanese corporation known as Recruit Holdings.[12]

Founded in 1960, Recruit originally operated in a field that is now almost extinct: it was an advertising agency that specialized in placing help-wanted notices in newspapers, particularly papers aimed at student readers. Today, Recruit has grown into an international corporation with footholds in a wide array of businesses—testimony to the company's ability to continually innovate its business model in response to shifts in technology, markets, and customer needs. With some 366 subsidiaries in over 60 countries that employ more than 49,000 people, Recruit Holdings boasts annual revenues of more than $16 billion, with about 40 percent coming from operations outside of Japan (all data as of March 2020). Since 2010, Recruit has been active in the United States, beginning with acquisitions of staffing companies including CSI, Staffmark Group, and Indeed. In 2018, it purchased Glassdoor, the well-known website where employees can provide anonymous information about the experience of working at particular companies. Recruit's business activities range from magazines and websites that deliver information about jobs, travel, real estate, restaurants, and other topics, to corporate staffing services and used car sales.

The journey by which Recruit made its way into this broad swath of industries has been driven both by external trends and an internal culture of opportunistic innovation. For example, in the 1960s, when thousands of Japanese college graduates found jobs through the on-campus recruiting efforts of major corporations, Recruit noticed that smaller companies had no comparable channel for attracting talent. In response, Recruit launched *Kigyo e no Shotai* (*Invitation to Companies*), a magazine for students in which small companies could place their own recruitment ads. Similarly, in 1980, recognizing the difficulty that Japanese women had in finding a varied range of attractive job opportunities, Recruit founded *Travail* magazine (known in Japanese as *Torabayu*) to focus on female job hunters.

In the 1990s, with the rise of the internet, Recruit began shifting to online media. By 2005, it had created more than 200 websites that helped to connect customers to businesses, including restaurants, beauty salons, and spas. Little by little, Recruit had reframed itself from a traditional advertising agency into a digitally enabled platform business, willing to provide services to customers wherever the need for a convenient online connection hub was apparent. Recruit now defines its business as being centered on matching platforms related either to "life event" activities (such as finding a new job, buying a car or a house, or getting married) or "lifestyle" activities (like booking a hotel or a hairstyling).[13] Recruit continues to provide other companies with the human resource services it has offered since its founding, with a focus on helping clients improve their productivity through cloud-based services and tools.

To make its impressive growth and diversification possible, Recruit consciously defined itself as a company centered on innovation. Founder Hiromasa Ezoe developed the slogan "Create your own opportunities and let the opportunities change yourself," which became one of the company's touchstone concepts. Business professor Howard Yu has studied Recruit's culture and describes it this way:

> Anybody in Recruit can be an innovator. No matter what function or task you play, you should never rest on the status quo, you should have the courage to see if a particular process is really needed, if there is any room for more productivity, if more value can be added to a particular component of the value chain. Outstanding sense of ownership shall lead to continuous improvement in daily work. Go beyond the scope of your own company, and carefully scrutinize other areas and industries, their life cycles and activities in doing so.[14]

On a regular basis, Recruit employees are challenged to define their jobs in terms of the personal values they feel passionate about, using the question, Why are you here? The goal is to help Recruit attract a cadre of highly motivated, innovation-minded frontline employees. This creates the potential for continuous innovation at Recruit. To turn this potential into reality, Recruit has empowered its midlevel management team to support and develop the creative thinking of employees in a number of powerful ways.

One of these is managing and promoting Ring, Recruit's system for attracting, evaluating, and developing new business proposals. Launched in 1982, it is currently an annual contest organized by Ring's corporate planning office. Among the businesses that originated as Ring entries are Zexy (a magazine and an online site providing brides with information on everything from wedding venues to gowns and jewelry), R25 (a magazine and website tailored for businesspeople age 25 and up), and Study Sapuri (an online study course platform that offers coaching services for students, teachers, and others). Another innovation system in which Recruit's midlevel coaches play a leading role is Forum, an annual event that honors novel practices that bring improvements to the company's existing businesses. Forum awards are given in four categories—client relationships, IT and other technology, product development and improvement, and business foundation.

It's not just the managers in charge of specialized programs who take innovating seriously. The same attitude pervades the entire organization. It's vividly illustrated by the story behind one of the company's newest businesses.[15]

B-MATCH is an offshoot of Recruit's CarSensor business, which itself was launched in 1984 as a magazine to connect used-car dealers with consumers. Over more than 35 years, CarSensor has been a fount of innovation for the Japanese used-car industry. In 1997, in order to provide richer and more reliable information to used-car buyers, the magazine mandated that dealers had to begin displaying the odometer reader for vehicles in their advertisements. In 2000, CarSensor added a requirement that the car's repair history be revealed, and in 2004, it required the vehicle identification number as a way of eliminating the potential for bait-and-switch ads. Further innovations have included the creation in 2010 of a third-party inspection and evaluation system called CarSensor Certificate, and, in 2012, the establishment of the industry's highest-standard after-sales service guarantee program. In 2017, CarSensor also began encouraging dealers to reveal the total cost of cars in their ads, including not just the sticker price but all the ancillary expenses involved; as of 2021, some 70 percent of the 490,000 ads run each year followed this guideline.

B-MATCH represents the newest innovation by the CarSensor division—and perhaps the most unusual. Rather than being a business-to-consumer (B2C) media business, it's a business-to-business (B2B) platform that matches upstream companies (which buy used cars from customers, including new-car dealers) with downstream companies (which sell used cars to customers). It's a huge business, with a total market of some 1.2 trillion yen (over $11 billion). But it's also highly competitive: a number of intermediate companies have long occupied the space, mostly conducting auction sales for used cars as they become available. It's also a complex marketplace, in which four sets of stakeholder parties—auto manufacturers, new-car dealers, industry associations, and used-car dealers—are all influential and need to have their interests met. So perhaps it's not surprising that when Ryo Maeda, a frontline employee in the CarSensor division, initially proposed the idea to CarSensor president Masami Muro, he was turned down.

In most companies, the story might end there. But not at Recruit, and especially not at CarSensor. Muro is particularly dedicated to inspiring, training, and empowering his team members to make the most of their innovative powers. He communicates continually with frontline employees about divisional goals and strategies via meetings, departmental visits, and newsletters. He hosts two internal training programs, the School for Smartest (open to all) and the School for Genius (selection-based), which are designed to provide employees with the tools and skills they need to hone their innovative ideas.

Perhaps most important, Muro is known to be tenacious about supporting innovative ideas that he thinks have potential, even when they produce initial resistance. For example, back in 2004, the concept of including vehicle ID numbers to prevent bait-and-switch ads had angered some advertisers; a number of them actually withdrew their business from CarSensor, leading to a decline in ad sales revenues of some $9 million. But Muro knew it was the right thing to do for consumers. He stuck to his guns, and within a few years, CarSensor's business was stronger than ever.

So when Muro turned down Maeda's concept for a B2B business platform under the CarSensor brand, he didn't leave matters there. He was intrigued enough to spend time with Maeda reviewing the details of the proposal and offering specific suggestions for improvement. Other middle managers were invited to weigh in, and they also provided useful ideas. Maeda reworked his proposal and submitted it again . . . only to be turned down again. More coaching and further improvements followed—not once or twice but repeatedly. In the end, it took three years of experimentation for Maeda to develop a business plan that the entire CarSensor management team approved.

B-MATCH was finally launched in 2019. Now it is battling for its share of the $11 billion Japanese used-car auction market. And Muro sees it as just the opening gambit in a big new strategic direction for CarSensor. The mantra that Muro has now begun sharing with his colleagues is "Let's transform ourselves from a B2C media tool into a B2B platform and management support partner by 2023." It all happened because of a frontline innovator who wouldn't take no for an answer—and his boss, a midlevel coach who spent three years providing the feedback and support needed to get an innovative concept across the finish line.

●—●—●

The Allianz, IBM, and Recruit stories illustrate the important roles that midlevel managers play in innovating. Frontline workers are often the main source of innovative ideas—although midlevel managers, too, are frequently eager and able to generate ideas for innovations that can produce new forms of value for companies and their customers.

However, midlevel managers also have a unique job to do when it comes to innovating. As the "glue" that connects the company's top leadership with its frontline workers, as well as creating connections across functions, departments, and divisions, midlevel managers need to be prepared to support the innovative efforts of frontline workers through encouragement, coaching, advice, connections to other colleagues, and help in navigating the process of development and implementation. Companies with great track records of innovation are those with midlevel managers who are truly committed to devoting time, energy, and creativity to making sure the innovating engine keeps running at full speed.

KEY TAKEAWAYS FROM CHAPTER 7

- Within the innovating engine, *midlevel managers are particularly important in driving the integration process.*
- *Midlevel managers must help to organize and operate the system* that winnows, channels, develops, and ultimately launches innovative concepts.
- *Midlevel managers serve as innovating coaches and cheerleaders,* supporting frontline employees and encouraging them to keep the stream of new ideas flowing.
- *Midlevel managers play a key role in helping to connect the dots* between innovative ideas, the employees who generate those ideas, and key resources around the organization.
- When midlevel managers are engaged in supporting innovating on a continual basis, it helps to ensure that *innovating is a deep-rooted part of the organization's DNA.*

8

SETTING THE AGENDA

HOW SENIOR LEADERS CAN FOCUS AN ENTIRE ORGANIZATION ON INNOVATING

Professional sports is one of the most competitive business arenas in the world. Not only are teams required to compete for victories on the gridiron, on the diamond, or in the arena, but they must also compete for "share of mind" among customers who are free to spend their hours and dollars on an ever-expanding array of other entertainment options.

In North America, the National Hockey League (NHL) faces some of the toughest business challenges in sports. A distant fourth among America's "big four," it trails the National Football League, Major League Baseball, and the National Basketball Association in terms of in-person attendance, television viewing, and overall revenues. The sport's appeal also tends to be geographically limited. Professional hockey is dominated by a handful of successful franchises in cities with storied traditions in the sport, including the New York Rangers, Toronto Maple Leafs, Montreal Canadiens, and Boston Bruins. Other NHL teams, especially those in cities where ice hockey is relatively new and unfamiliar, struggle to attract fans, TV ratings, and coverage in the local sports media.

One of the NHL franchises facing a particularly tough set of challenges is the San Jose Sharks. Its home base in Northern California is no hockey hotbed. From 1967 to 1976, the region was represented in the NHL by the San Francisco Golden Seals. After a decade of struggles, that team gave up its attempt to gain a foothold in the area and moved to Cleveland, only to go out of business entirely just two years later.

NHL hockey returned to the area when the Sharks were founded in 1991. But like San Francisco, San Jose isn't naturally hospitable to ice hockey. Located in the heart of Silicon Valley, it's filled with hardworking families immersed in digital forms of entertainment. And because the city of San Jose has some of the worst rush-hour traffic anywhere, even getting to the games is an ordeal most people would prefer to skip.

Clearly, the task of building an enthusiastic, sustainable fan base for the Sharks is one that calls for more than the usual level of innovation.

Bringing a Culture of Innovating to the Tradition-Loving World of Pro Sports

Under the leadership of club president Jonathan Becher, formerly chief digital officer for the software company SAP, the San Jose Sharks have been finding unexpected ways to turn the franchise's apparent liabilities into assets. In the process, they've won a reputation as the most innovative organization in the NHL and one of the most innovative teams in all of professional sports. Northern Californians, in turn, have been responding by making the Sharks one of the fastest-growing franchises in the league.

The Sharks have accomplished all this in large part by applying the talent for digital innovation that Becher brought to the team's front office. For example, when the Sharks' marketing group found that as many as 40 percent of fans were showing up late for games—one of the problems caused by Silicon Valley's skyrocketing growth and the horrendous traffic jams it has generated—they developed digital tools to create countervailing incentives. One of these is an app that fans can use to track their arrival time at the team's downtown arena and then rewards early comers with a $10 discount on food and merchandise.

The Sharks have also devised additional interactive systems to increase fan engagement, including the world's first augmented reality bobblehead doll. This is a high-tech version of the traditional figurines that fans of every sport have long collected, this one equipped with a QR code that lets you experience "a day in the life" of the team's star forward Logan Couture.

Despite the Sharks' Silicon Valley location, such digital innovations didn't come naturally to them. When Becher joined the team in January 2018, he found that, like many sports franchises, the Sharks were somewhat tradition-bound and averse to experimentation. He made changing that mindset one of his chief missions.

Becher's background at SAP had prepared him well for this task. As that company's chief digital officer, one of his core missions was to help SAP's client companies embrace technological disruption, including the new ways of doing business that SAP itself was offering. Along the way, he learned a great deal about how and why companies find it difficult to accept change. He compared the tendency of business leaders to reject change to the mechanism by which the human body deploys antibodies to fight off a "foreign agent." "The same thing happens in large companies as well," Becher commented in an SAP company video. "When something seems to disrupt the current business model, the traditionalist will say, 'Hmm, that jeopardizes our revenue. We should maybe keep it from growing.'"[1]

"Traditionalists" who instinctively resist innovation are found in every successful organization, but professional sports is one industry where they have a particularly powerful foothold. Fans are steeped in the history of the sports they love. Memories of heroic athletes, beloved venues, and iconic moments shape their relationships with the teams they follow, and they pass the culture of fandom down to their children and grandchildren with some of the fervor of a religious obligation or a political passion. This tradition-laden love of the game permeates the industry itself, since most of the athletes as well as the managers and executives of professional sports organizations are themselves fans who grew up rooting for their favorite teams. No wonder they tend to be skeptical of innovations that might seem to threaten the culture they've grown up loving.

The classic book *Moneyball* by journalist Michael Lewis vividly captures the way iconoclastic thinkers who discover new ways to apply statistical analysis to sports then have to struggle to convince traditionalists to give their methods a try. Lewis's narrative focuses on Major League Baseball, but a similar dynamic can be found in all of the major pro sports, including hockey. The dominant culture of the sports industry is focused on honoring, even worshiping, the past, not on imagining a different future. Thus, sports leaders who hope to innovate have an even bigger cultural challenge than their counterparts in most other arenas.

After joining the Sharks, Becher tackled the culture-change challenge from several angles. One of the approaches he took was to invite those who were most resistant to change to participate in creating it and designing it for scale. "By centralizing disruption and not putting it on the edge," Becher observes, "you're more likely to be successful." He emphasized the need for a hands-on approach to innovation, particularly in the world of sports. "Normally large companies look for experts when they have problems," Becher said, "and those experts often come from the outside of the organization; consultants." But relying on outsiders to generate change can stimulate the production of even more change-resistant antibodies. A better approach, Becher realized, was to teach company insiders how to devise their own innovative approaches. In the process, the organizational culture begins to shift, making innovating feel natural rather than foreign.

Becher also inculcated a focus on running multiple innovating experiments—placing many small bets on new ideas rather than one or two giant bets. This approach has made his team members more willing to embrace innovation by minimizing the risk involved in trying any single idea, instead providing multiple opportunities to discover something new that will really work.

But perhaps the most important culture-shifting strategy that Becher employed was encouraging the leadership team in the Sharks organization to think about innovation not as a disruption of the fan experience they all loved, but rather as a way to enhance and deepen it. For example, when seeking to broaden the definition of the company's business model, he explained it this way: "I don't think we're in the business of putting on a hockey game. What we're actually in the business of is making memories."[2] That's a formulation any dyed-in-the-wool sports fan can understand and embrace.

Becher went on to educate his team about the importance of developing a fan-centered innovating engine alongside the existing execution engine, describing it like this: "It's flipping your mindset from internal, business process functionality—operation-oriented—to what customers need. If we go back to business books written 20, 30 years ago, it's the modern version of walking a mile in their shoes."

Becher's commitment to the customer point of view is so deep that he even took the radical step of urging his front-office colleagues to focus on nurturing the passion of their fans even when their efforts did not result in an immediate or direct boost to revenues. In an interview, Becher explained, "My worry when I did this in the past with my colleagues is the customer journey always had the outcome of, 'How do we sell them something?' And so, if I give you very tactical advice, it's building customer journeys that don't always have the outcome of having them buy something."[3]

Thus, encouraging fans to arrive at the games early isn't just about having them buy more snacks and souvenirs—it's about deepening their connection with the sport and the team. It allows them to experience the full arc of the game, from the ceremonial dropping of the first puck to the final buzzer. It also gives them time to enjoy the various special features of the 17,000-seat SAP Center, which fans have lovingly dubbed "The Shark Tank," such as its state-of-the-art digital display screens. Becher is convinced that innovating on behalf of customers—in his case, fans of the Sharks—will always have an ultimate payoff, even if it's not obvious in the short term.

Becher's nurturing of an innovation-centric culture in the team's front office became more important than ever in 2020, when pro sports suffered an unprecedented level of disruption thanks to the worldwide COVID-19 pandemic. In April, when all of the big four sports in North America had to stop playing in public because of the pandemic, it was the first time that none of the American pro leagues had been open for business in April since 1883.[4]

The pro hockey shutdown posed a potentially franchise-threatening challenge to every NHL team, including the Sharks. How could the team maintain its bond with the fans when it could no longer provide them with the adrenaline-pumping excitement of games to watch, either in person or on TV? The danger was that, after weeks or months without hockey, the fans would discover other forms of entertainment they liked almost as much, and perhaps lose the hockey habit altogether.

To keep that from happening, the Sharks redoubled their innovative efforts.

One of the things they decided to try—at first out of sheer desperation—was using a video-game simulation platform to put on "fantasy" hockey games for fans to watch. Today's popular sports simulation software combines statistical analysis of real-life hockey players with randomized play-by-play events to show what might happen in a game between, say, the Sharks and the Dallas Stars or the Vancouver Canucks. Hockey-crazy fans enjoy playing these simulated games on their sofas at home, but they would never be considered an adequate replacement for the real sport—except under the extreme circumstances created by the pandemic.

When the real-world 2020 season was suspended, the Sharks (and other pro sports teams) began televising computer-generated simulated games, using actual video clips of their players to make the action look almost real. They were pleasantly surprised to find that their fans actually liked watching the simulated games. The TV ratings didn't match those of the real sport, but they weren't bad.

And then the Sharks began applying their talent for innovating to this unexpected new opportunity. They introduced one new wrinkle after another to turn the fan experience of the simulated games into something truly special.

Perhaps the most exciting of these innovations was the idea of giving selected fans the opportunity to "suit up" and play alongside their favorite Sharks players. When a fan was picked from the pool of avid applicants, the software designed an avatar to mimic that fan's size and appearance, and decked the fan out in a uniform complete with personalized name and number. Then the Sharks sent the avatar out on the ice to play a game under the control of the joy-stick-equipped fan.

The result was a collection of simulated experiences that Sharks fans have found unforgettable. The very first avatar to play in a Sharks game actually suffered an "injury" during the action (as dictated by the random rules of the software) and had to be removed from the game. At first, the fan was devastated and angry, screaming, "Unfair!" at this unhappy turn of events. But after the avatar was carried into the locker room by his virtual teammates—and after the team's general manager Doug Wilson placed a real-world phone call to the fan to deliver a "get well" message—the fan described the whole experience as, "Definitely a highlight of 2020 and a moment I won't soon forget." Another fan had the thrill of scoring the game-winning goal during an overtime game and celebrating on the ice with his excited teammates. He took to social media to declare it "the best experience of his life."

Delighted by these fan responses, the Sharks went on to introduce further innovations to the simulated hockey experience. They began inserting simulated versions of popular Sharks players from past eras into the games, making possible the kinds of fantasy matchups across history that sports fans have always loved to dream and argue about. They also engaged the team's popular radio play-by-play announcer, Dan Rusanowsky, to narrate the action of the simulated games, lending them a realism and an excitement that the fans really responded to.

This development of simulated pro hockey as a way of extending and deepening the fan experience happened only because of the emergency circumstances created by COVID-19. But the value of the innovation won't disappear when the pandemic is history. Although detailed plans for the use of simulated games in future seasons haven't yet been made, Becher believes this new way of involving fans will be "sticky." "The games might be simulated," Becher says, "but the fan engagement is real."

Becher didn't personally dream up these brilliant sporting innovations—in fact, he was surprised at their power, because he himself doesn't play video hockey. But Becher led the way in creating the culture of innovating that unleashed the inventive genius of the entire Sharks organization, including its digital creativity. No wonder one technology vendor with ties to a number of pro hockey teams has commented, "Oh, in the NHL, everyone looks to the San Jose Sharks for the way they engage the fans now."[5]

Levers of Innovation That the CEO Can Control

The story of Becher's work with the San Jose Sharks illustrates one of the most important roles that a top-level executive can play in a business—namely, to jump-start the innovating engine. When an organization is lagging its competition due to a failure to innovate; when it is struggling to adapt to changes in its business environment, the needs of its customers, or the technological underpinnings of its industry; or when it is unable to take full advantage of business opportunities because of excessive rigidity, risk-aversion, or blind spots—in any of these circumstances, a single leader at the top of the organization can sometimes exert his or her personal leverage to start a cascading series of cultural and organizational changes that can get the flywheel of innovation spinning.

Of course, like anyone in an organization, at any position in the company hierarchy or in any specific functional role, a CEO, president, executive vice president, board chair, or other top leader is expected to be a contributor of innovating ideas. The process of creation is one that everyone can participate in. But top leaders also have a unique job to do in stimulating and encouraging innovating throughout the organization. They carry out this catalytic role through the influence they exert on three main levers:

> ▶ *Lever 1: The organizational structure.* The leader can work to promote innovating by advocating and implementing changes in the formal structure, rules, and guidelines that govern the organization. For example, leaders can appoint one or more executives to roles that are focused on innovating; they can create committees or teams charged with stimulating the development of innovative ideas and shepherding them through the evaluation and implementation steps; and they can support and contribute to the

creation of systems and networks that facilitate teamwork and cocreation across departments and divisions of the organization.

▶ *Lever 2: Key organizational processes.* The leader can work with others to redefine the processes carried out by people, teams, and departments throughout the organization, making sure that time, money, energy, attention, and other resources are dedicated to innovating. A leader can also promote revisions to the organization's hiring, evaluation, and promotion processes that incentivize and reward innovating.

▶ *Lever 3: The organizational culture.* The leader can use his or her power, influence, and "bully pulpit" to move the shared values, beliefs, and attitudes that shape the organization in the direction of fostering and protecting innovating. Leaders can "give permission to innovate" to people throughout the organization through actions such as publicly recognizing and rewarding those who develop innovations, shielding from punishment or criticism those who take risks and incur reasonable levels of failure in pursuit of innovating, and using their own communication tools to spread the word about the value and importance of innovating. Perhaps most important, CEOs should reposition themselves as their companies' "Chief Reframing Officers" by personally modeling leadership traits that nurture innovating: open-mindedness, transparency, customer-centricity, listening, and a willingness to experiment.

In many cases, a company's top leaders can do a lot to stimulate innovating simply through *negative* steps—that is, by eliminating needless obstacles and barriers that discourage risk-taking, experimentation, and creativity. Frontline employees and midlevel managers in most companies are eager to innovate. Many are in close contact with customers, deeply engaged in the daily activities of the business, and full of ideas about how the company's products, services, and processes could be improved. All they lack is the organizational freedom and encouragement to act on their innovative dreams. Once that freedom is provided, they are thrilled to be able to unleash their creative ideas.

Innovating activities can go a long way to increasing your employees' sense of engagement with their work and their positive attitudes toward the organization. Being able to innovate lifts people out of their daily immersion in execution tasks, which often feels routine and uninspiring. Innovating brings richness and fun to work, stimulating team members to spend more time with both customers and noncustomers, and encouraging them to listen mindfully to the subtle messages that the marketplace is trying to deliver.

If you are at or near the top of your organizational pyramid, you should begin taking steps to encourage, legitimize, and support innovating by everyone in your business. If you begin sending the clear, consistent messages that innovating is part of everyone's job and that innovation is core to your company's strategy, you may be amazed by the torrent of creative ideas that will begin to flow.

Turning Executive Management into a Dynamo of Innovation: Leadership from the Top at Ecocem

As we've seen, Jonathan Becher is an example of a new breed of corporate leaders who are deliberately focusing on the cultural challenge of innovation as a key to the future of their businesses. His work with the San Jose Sharks shows how an innovation-minded leader at the top can help make an organization in a tradition-minded industry into a powerhouse of creativity.

Even more remarkably, something similar can happen in practically every business.

In Chapter 3, we sketched the story of Ecocem, the fast-growing European cement maker. It was founded by entrepreneur Donal O'Riain to take advantage of an underused technological innovation—ground granulated blast furnace slag (GGBS), a cement substitute with a much smaller carbon footprint than conventional cement as well as other benefits. We saw how Ecocem has developed an unusual degree of customer intimacy, which has enabled it to produce a range of product and service innovations that are generating enormous value both for its customers and for Ecocem itself.

The creation of this powerful innovating engine didn't happen by itself. It was driven from the top, starting with O'Riain. The story of how it happened offers some powerful lessons that other company leaders can benefit from.[6]

One of the big challenges O'Riain faced in turning Ecocem into a leader of innovation was the dominant culture of the cement industry. As we saw in Chapter 3, the industry is an old one, steeped in tradition and largely controlled by a handful of giant companies that occupy powerful positions with stable shares of a profitable market. For Ecocem to claim its own share of that market, it needed to develop an innovating culture quite different from the one that characterized its biggest competitors. The challenges in creating such a culture started at the very top, with Ecocem's board of directors.

The members of this board were smart, experienced, and knowledgeable about the cement industry. Perhaps for this very reason, they were skeptical when O'Riain told them that Ecocem needed to become an innovation-driven company, beginning with making a commitment to devote 2 percent of its revenues to innovating. "The board members thought I was a bit daft," O'Riain recalls. "They asked, 'Is that really necessary?' I insisted that it was. And I realized that I needed to convert them into innovation enthusiasts."

The conversion process began with education. In 2016, to spearhead the effort, O'Riain set up a special technology subcommittee that includes several members of the board of directors. It meets twice a year with four or five key managers of Ecocem who are immersed in the company's most important innovating projects, including Laurent Frouin, the innovation director. The group spends half a day together delving deeply into six or seven key innovation topics, gaining a hands-on understanding of Ecocem's current research and development (R&D) projects and why they are so important to the company's future. The board members' level of technological expertise has risen significantly, to the point where they can now ask probing questions of the engineers and scientists they meet with as well as share ideas of their own that may be valuable. They can also provide detailed, convincing responses when their fellow board members question the value of Ecocem's investments in innovating.

The members of the technology subcommittee also perform an in-depth review of the financial results being obtained from the company's innovation budget. O'Riain explains that Ecocem is currently spending some €2 million per year (equal to almost $2.5 million) on innovating—"a frugal approach," he says, but a sum sufficient to ensure that the innovating engine continues to hum. The cumulative return on investment has increased steadily over time and now runs between 30 and 40 percent annually. It's a figure the board takes very seriously. "The fact that we can point to a solid ROI on the money we spend on innovating has turned the skeptics on our board into cheerleaders," O'Riain says. He hopes the ROI on innovating will continue to grow, estimating that it may reach as high as 60 percent annually by 2025.

The benefits of having a technology subcommittee on the board of directors run in both directions. The board members have taken a big upward leap in their knowledge of innovating processes in the cement business, which enables them to make smarter decisions about how to invest the company's funds and how to shape its marketplace strategies to take full advantage of emerging opportunities. For their part, the engineers, scientists, and managers who meet twice a year with the board members have also gained a lot. They've developed personal connections and lines of communication to some of the most important people in the organization, which is always helpful. They've sharpened their understanding of how innovation looks to leaders at the highest level of the cement industry, which helps them think about their work in strategic terms as well as technological terms. And realizing that they have enthusiastic followers and supporters among the members of the board has intensified their personal commitment to the pursuit of innovating.

"Our R&D team is now more motivated than ever," O'Riain says, "especially when it comes to looking for great applications of the new ideas they think up."

Ecocem took further steps to spread the new innovation-centric company culture throughout all levels of the organization. With O'Riain's support, consultant Maria Beloso Hall, an expert in behavioral transformation and change management, was brought in to coach company leaders in ways to encourage everyone to participate in the innovating process. In one team, she found that a handful of highly confident engineers with degrees from the leading French engineering universities were inadvertently intimidating some of the people they worked with, including a group of lab technicians whose credentials were less impressive. Hall organized a "collective intelligence" training program that helped the entire team understand that everyone has valuable insights, ideas, and questions that can benefit the shared effort. As a result, every team member gained a greater willingness to speak up during meetings, thereby surfacing problems and issues more quickly and making the process of generating, developing, and testing innovating ideas more effective.

Ecocem offers a great example of how an organizational leader can make sure that regular activities in support of innovating are embedded in the routine processes of the business, thereby ensuring that no one loses sight of the centrality of innovating for the company's future.

The culture of innovating has become so central to Ecocem that it is now the first word in the company's motto: "Innovation Powering Sustainability." That's a powerful public symbol of what can happen when a company's board is encouraged to put innovating at the center of its thinking.

When the Company's Highest Leaders Show the Way

As the stories we've explored in this chapter suggest, one of the most important jobs of CEOs and their leadership teams is to model the readiness to pursue and embrace innovations. That means being willing to challenge familiar orthodoxies, habits, and traditions, and to change beliefs and behaviors as needed to create new value for the organization and its customers—rather than reacting to innovation with suspicion, defensiveness, or hostility.

At many companies that have adopted the innovation methods I teach, the CEO and the entire board have led the way by being the first group to go through our full training process. The leadership team should also use all available corporate communication channels to explain and legitimize the distinction between execution and innovating, and to encourage all employees to spend time in the innovating space.

Symbolic actions by top leadership can carry enormous weight throughout the organization. When the BASF board of directors launched its Perspectives project to teach and promote innovation, it made the announcement at a public meeting in front of 1,500 employees—which not only got the attention of all the leading managers at BASF but also signaled the board's personal commitment to the concept of innovation at all levels of the business.

Occasionally, corporations that are launching an innovation initiative will assign a human resources (HR) professional to run it. This can be a serious misstep. Managers from HR and other staff departments (such as corporate communications) are often regarded by their colleagues as less powerful, knowledgeable, and effective than managers who are responsible for building businesses measured in terms of profit-and-loss results. Such staff managers may be taken seriously in training roles, but their ability to transform the attitudes and behaviors of their colleagues is limited. As one consultant with extensive experience in fostering a culture of innovation told me, "As soon as the CEO or executive committee member stops participating in the initiative, it becomes just another training exercise, and before long it fades away."[7]

BASF avoided this mistake. The executive tasked with heading Perspectives and organizing the teams of coaches and ambassadors who brought its message of innovation to the rest of the organization was a highly respected manager with years of operating experience at BASF. As a marketing specialist and a former head of corporate procurement, Andrés Jaffé had been an internal customer who had worked closely with managers in many departments and divisions of BASF. His operational expertise and his in-depth understanding of BASF and its businesses were unquestioned. By choosing Jaffé for this role, the corporation signaled the seriousness of its commitment to it.

John Feldman, a member of the board, was designated as the official sponsor for the Perspectives initiative. In that role, he provided the project with credibility and legitimacy. He also protected and defended it within the board and across the entire corporation, communicating its importance and explaining why the time, money, and other resources dedicated to it were of crucial importance to the future of BASF. And throughout the years-long process of embedding innovating behaviors at every layer of the organization, when employees at all the BASF divisions were asked to attend workshops and meetings to master the

Perspectives approach, at least one board member made a point of attending every session—yet another sign of the seriousness attached to the effort.

When the top leaders of an organization use their words and actions to consistently demonstrate the urgency of innovation, they help to create a culture of innovating that will eventually energize the entire organization.

KEY TAKEAWAYS FROM CHAPTER 8

- In building the company's innovating engine, *senior leaders need to become their companies' "chief reframing officers,"* modeling openness to change and the questioning of familiar assumptions.
- Senior leaders must dedicate themselves to inculcating the spirit of innovating throughout the organization, especially using the three most powerful levers of influence at their disposal: *the organizational structure, organizational processes,* and *organizational culture.*
- To further signal the seriousness of the organization's commitment to innovating, senior leaders should themselves be *among the first to adopt innovating systems and practices.*
- Senior leaders must also emphasize the urgency of innovating by assigning *widely respected, high-level leaders with operational expertise* to spearhead the organization's innovating efforts.

PART FOUR

THE INFRASTRUCTURE FOR INNOVATING GOVERNANCE AND COORDINATION

9

IGNITING
THE ENGINE

CREATING A GOVERNANCE AND
COORDINATION STRUCTURE FOR
THE INNOVATING ENGINE

f you were playing a word association game, the top response
to "Bayer" would be inevitable—"aspirin." The 150-year-old
company is best known for its development and marketing
of acetylsalicylic acid, the miracle drug developed by Bayer
chemists in the 1890s and originally trademarked worldwide as
aspirin. But though aspirin is still a mainstay of Bayer's business, the $40 billion company also profits from a steady stream
of innovations in pharmacology and the life sciences: for example, technologies that help smallholder farmers in developing
countries expand their production of sustainable crops; artificial
intelligence (AI) software designed to improve clinical decision-
making regarding chronic conditions like hypertension; and

breakthrough treatments for medical conditions ranging from hemophilia to prostate cancer. These examples reflect just a few recent months of Bayer research.

Breakthroughs like these reflect the degree to which Bayer recognizes the centrality of innovation to its future success. The company operates according to a mantra that was explained to me by Dr. Henning Trill, one of Bayer's innovating leaders and head of Corporate Innovation: "When running a sustainable business, innovation and marketing are critical. They cannot be outsourced and they can't be delegated to others. Even though innovation often calls for cooperation and partnership with outside stakeholders, such as business partners, academic research organizations, biotech companies, medical institutions, and many kinds of customers, the innovating process itself *must* be driven from within—because otherwise, the company runs the risk of losing control of its destiny."

Of course, Bayer's stream of business-building innovations depends fundamentally on the ideas generated by scientists, engineers, and researchers in dozens of Bayer laboratories around the world, as well as other technical experts in companies that partner with Bayer. But *ideas* are just the beginning. In the words of Dr. Monika Lessl, Bayer's head of Corporate Innovation, R&D and Social Innovation, who leads the organization's innovation efforts: "Ideas are cheap! We've learned creation is not enough. . . . The idea is critical, but the translation to bring it to life and our understanding of the underlying problem is where we often fail. We often love our solutions or technologies and don't invest enough time and energy to search for the real customer or patient need. That's why innovation leadership is different from other kinds of leadership. The first is both a product of a purposely created environment and the cause to make ideas happen."

The "purposely created environment" that Bayer has developed to keep "making ideas happen" adds up to a powerful—and thoughtfully designed—innovating engine.[1]

How Bayer Encourages Innovators: WeSolve and Beyond

As Bayer's 150-year track record suggests, the company has been innovating for a long time. But as the world evolves, so must business methods and strategies, and this applies to innovating as much as to other practices. Bayer's contemporary journey of innovating began with what Monika Lessl calls "a white sheet of paper" in 2014, when the company realized it needed to provide its many widely dispersed worldwide employees with better ways to innovate—faster, more agile, more open-ended. "We had a hundred thousand people around the world, all wondering, 'How can I contribute to innovation?'" says Dr. Lessl. "This resource offered us immense potential. We asked ourselves, 'How can we leverage it?'"

One crucial piece of the answer related to Bayer's corporate structure. Bayer is a huge company, with employees in three major business divisions (pharmaceuticals, consumer health, and crop science) scattered across 36 country groups around the world. Inevitably, such a company must be organized along hierarchical lines, with the bureaucratic systems and procedures needed to maintain control and strategic focus while engaging in hundreds of thousands of separate activities. Yet bureaucracy can easily become a deadening influence that stifles innovation.

Dr. Lessl and her team were inspired by the organizational model of John Kotter, well-known management theorist. He has spoken and written extensively about how organizations can develop *dual systems* that combine traditional vertical hierarchies with more flexible, horizontally structured networks in order to facilitate freewheeling interaction, communication, and collaboration. They decided they needed to find a way to create such a dual structure in support of their employees' innovating efforts.

Notice that the duality Kotter and others have recommended is closely related to the concept of the two engines that I've presented in this book. The hierarchical structure most big companies have inherited from their history is strongly aligned with the execution engine that performs crucial daily functions. The horizontal network needed to open up channels of communications among people in various functions and departments is aligned with the innovating engine that fosters creativity. The question is, How to operate both engines simultaneously, and not as separate units with different personnel but with the involvement and support of *everyone* in the organization?

During a strategy project in 2015, the innovation team led by Dr. Lessl decided to develop a horizontal network dedicated to innovating that would invite the creative participation of everyone in the company. Then the company would find ways to feed the ideas fostered by this network back into the hierarchical execution system.

In creating such a network, managers would play a crucial role. Dr. Trill explains why:

> When we started the Innovation Agenda, I thought I could spur innovation by asking the company's senior leaders to name their three biggest problems. Then I would turn to Bayer people at all levels to find solutions. But that didn't work. The questions asked were too big and needed a further breakdown to be solvable. We had to systematically reach out to the organization via the Innovation Network to identify the right type of challenges that would trigger new solutions and even business models.
>
> The people in the country organizations are much closer to the challenges of the customers. They were essential to finding issues like, "Farmers in Spain want a way to monitor the pesticide levels in their crops at harvest time, and, even better, a way to predict those levels so they adjust their planting methods accordingly." The local managers and

frontline employees are the people who are in touch with customers and aware of their needs, issues, concerns, and wants. And they are the people who are not only willing to use creative problem-solving tools to innovate solutions but to actually experiment with those solutions until they find something that really adds value to the customer and for which the customer is willing to pay.

Originally the process of unearthing the countless challenges that Bayer people needed to address started with the launch of an online idea forum called WeSolve. This is a digital platform where Bayer employees from around the world are invited to post challenges, problems, and opportunities that they recognize from their local businesses. Other employees who visit the forum can then propose ideas for solutions. It's a kind of internal crowdsourcing tool that lets Bayer people from everywhere meet with one another in virtual space, bringing their unique experiences, knowledge, and insights to bear on far-flung issues they'd otherwise never hear about.

WeSolve quickly became a popular visiting place for Bayer employees. Within a year of its creation, more than 23,000 of Bayer's 100,000+ team members had visited the forum, and some 1,650 had contributed either challenges or possible solutions. Over time, fascinating and valuable new uses were developed for the forum. Not only technical or scientific solutions were sought. When Bayer's human resources division developed a new performance appraisal system, WeSolve was used as a platform for soliciting feedback from many of the company's most engaged and thoughtful employees. When volunteers were needed to serve as early testers for new Bayer products or services, WeSolve turned out to be an effective way of recruiting them. When product marketers needed feedback on their plans from people who represent the potential customer base (arthritis sufferers, for example) they discovered they could turn to

WeSolve to find such people among Bayer's worldwide employee base. When Bayer seeks an outside partner—another company, a nonprofit organization, or an academic institution—to provide the specialized skills or tools required to support a nascent project, WeSolve participants are invited to contribute suggestions and connections.

Additional innovation forums have also been created with specialized mandates. Some of these invite users to post ideas or solutions rather than challenges. One of these is called WeIdeate, a subforum within WeSolve. This forum focuses on specific activity areas or local problems. This is a deliberate strategy. Bayer has found that posting ideas works best within a small universe of people who share common issues and concerns. Outside this sort of limited setting, it is much less useful. As Dr. Trill observes, "Posting *ideas* in a broad-based online forum usually leads nowhere because there's not much chance that the person who owns the underlying problem will see the idea and then jump to adopt it. In a general-interest forum, it's much more effective to post challenges because then the potential solutions that people post in response have a built-in constituency."

Of all the Bayer forums dedicated to innovating, WeSolve has proved to be the one with the greatest impact and staying power. As of fall 2020, more than 40,000 Bayer people have participated on WeSolve. Considering that WeSolve is entirely in English, and only about 50,000 of Bayer's employees speak English, that's a very impressive rate of engagement.

More than 200 problem-solving challenges are now being posted on the forum every year. When I visited the WeSolve forum in mid-2020, I was impressed by the number and variety of issues it featured, all raised by Bayer employees for potential solution by others. Some posed problems that were quite technical: "We are looking for an additional safety measure to improve our dust-free big bag filling process." "Looking for ideas for improving germination rate and consistency across a variety of weed seeds." "We are looking for a suitable genome/variant graph algorithm for crops." Others were almost philosophical or even playful—for example, a survey on the topic "Is transparency in what you eat important to you?" and another asking for creative suggestions for a brand name for a new product for the Indian market. Scanning the dozens of challenges posed, I got the feeling that contributing to the WeSolve forum would actually be *fun* for Bayer employees. This is probably one of the main reasons the participation rate is so high.

Perhaps most impressive, the average number of visitors to any challenge or request appearing on the forum is about 200. Post a problem on WeSolve, and the odds of attracting a smart solution are quite high. Dr. Trill estimates that about 50 percent of WeSolve problems get solved outright, while in another 30 percent of cases a fresh idea or insight pointing toward a "workaround" is generated. And many of the best ideas come from unexpected sources. Dr. Trill reports that two-thirds of the best solutions come from people in a division or functional area different from the one where the person raising the issue works, reinforcing the value of WeSolve as a tool for companywide intelligence sharing.

Bayer's Dr. Julia Hitzbleck says, "Often, challenges we post are not solved by someone from that department or function, but from someone in a totally different division. It has really helped us to tap into our knowledge pool, and get into the spirit of working together rather than experts sticking to their own area."[2]

Dr. Trill points out another benefit of WeSolve's broad appeal: "When new employees join Bayer, whether as individuals or as part of a company acquisition, they find that WeSolve is a great way to discover what is happening throughout the business. Reading about challenges faced by Bayer people around the world and even being able to participate in solving them helps to glue the organization together." The fact that Bayer is being "glued together" around innovating makes it all doubly powerful and beneficial.

The Corporate I-Team:
Spark Plug of Innovating

Encouraged by the success of the WeSolve forum, Dr. Lessl and her team decided to spread their new way of innovating to Bayer employees across the organization. To make this happen, they began to build a network of coaches that would play a crucial role.

Throughout this book, I've stressed the fact that every employee in an organization has a role to play in innovating. It's important to break away from the traditional belief that innovation is the province only of a handful of creative geniuses with special talents and a unique role in the organization. The existence of the thriving WeSolve forum certainly sends a clear message to Bayer people that everyone is encouraged to contribute to creating the company's future.

However, it's also very helpful for an organization to have a cadre of employees who play special roles in encouraging and maintaining the flow of innovations through all three processes—creation, integration, and reframing. In particular, I recommend creating three new jobs to be assigned on either a full-time or part-time basis to particular members of your organizational team—the *innovating coach* (or *I-Coach*), the *innovating coordinator* (*I-Coordinator*), and the *innovating committee* (*I-Committee*). These three sets of individuals play important roles in reinforcing the culture of innovating in your organization.

Taken together, all the people who fill these jobs make up what I call the *innovating team,* or *I-Team* for short. Bayer offers a great example of how to build an I-Team and use it effectively to stimulate innovating throughout the organization.

Note that most members of your I-Team, like other members of your organization, will play differing roles at different times, depending on whether they are operating as part of the execution engine or as part of the innovating engine.

Figure 9.1 illustrates the similarities and differences between the twin engines and their organizational structures. Figure 9.1A depicts, in simplified form, a typical hierarchical structure like the one that most organizations use to govern their execution engine. Connections among the individuals in the chart are depicted by horizontal and vertical lines.

In Figure 9.1B, the formal structure of the organization's innovating engine is depicted. In this figure, the same individuals are shown, with the exception of a new box on the top righthand side of the chart. This box represents a special unit of I-Trainers who work with the I-Committee and train people throughout the organization in innovating methods, in particular the I-Coaches. The I-Trainers also serve as a central intelligence unit that prospects for, evaluates, and selects novel innovation methodologies and techniques as they emerge in the external market. They may also develop proprietary, customized processes for use by those within the organization who seek to innovate.

The other members of the I-Team—including the members of the I-Committee, the I-Coordinators, and the I-Coaches— are embedded throughout the organization at various levels and represented by boxes in differing shades of gray. Also notice the diagonal lines used to connect these I-Team members, reflecting the kind of cross-functional, multi-level teamwork that is characteristic of activities within an innovating engine. As the figure suggests, these connections may be quite different from the ones that exist within the traditional hierarchy that generally characterizes the execution engine.

Of course, every company will adapt the design of its I-Team to fit its culture, size, divisional structure, and other characteristics. Bayer, for example, started by giving an individual member of Bayer's executive board (i.e., its board of directors) a special responsibility for encouraging and supporting innovating. This was Kemal Malik. He set up a group under Dr. Lessl's leadership to develop an innovation strategy and define measures for implementation.

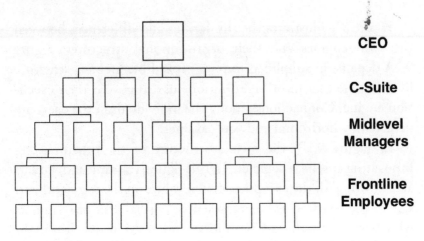

FIGURE 9.1A   Hierarchical Roles Within the Execution Engine

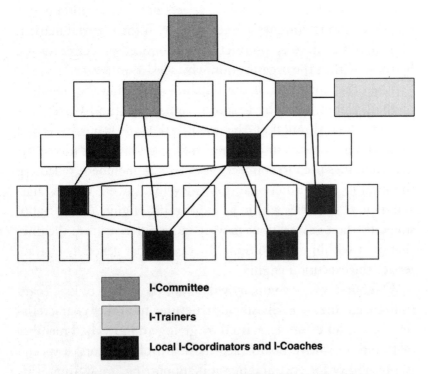

FIGURE 9.1B   Nonhierarchical Roles and Connections
Within the Innovating Engine

A key element of the strategy was to set up a cross-divisional innovation committee of senior executives. Furthermore, covering all country groups and global functions, 80 senior managers were selected to play the role of I-Coordinators, bearing the Bayer-specific designation "innovation ambassadors."

Finally, a third group of specialists was created, even bigger than the first two. At Bayer, these were called *innovation coaches*; I refer to them as I-Coaches. Between 2016 and 2020, more than 1,000 innovation coaches were trained, of which about 600 are still at work in Bayer facilities around the world. About 200 additional employees eager to join the team have placed their names on a waiting list.

I-Coaches are individuals trained and certified by the I-Trainers after participating in a corporatewide specific training program that may involve physical classes, virtual training sessions, or a combination of both. Through the training, they learn to use creative methods and tools like those I've mentioned throughout this book (and which I'll discuss in some detail in Chapter 10). Additional innovating methods that the I-Trainers have developed or adopted may also be included in the innovating curriculum. At Bayer, for example, I-Coaches take part in a three-day onboarding program that includes the detailed study of a technique called Systematic Inventive Thinking®, which they often use with their colleagues as a way of stimulating and organizing their innovating activities.

The I-Coach also works with innovating project teams or individual innovators in a particular part of the organization, helping them to understand how to apply the tools most effectively, troubleshooting their innovation efforts and linking them to other innovation-related support mechanisms at Bayer in order to help them make innovating a regular and productive part of their work.

One of the most effective activities sponsored by Bayer's I-Coaches is what the company calls *fast sessions*—short workshops with teams of four to six participants designed to address a specific problem, such as the need to simplify an overly complex process or to meet a competitor's challenge. These workshops have become very popular as they are easy to set up and fun to do.

In addition to fast sessions, the I-Coaches organize and lead one- to three-hour cocreation workshops, which often include individuals from outside organizations, such as business partners or Bayer customers. I-Coaches also hold informal "lunch and learn" gatherings at which innovative ideas from various companies and industries are presented and discussed. Through these cross-functional, sometimes interorganizational meetings, the I-Coaches are helping to support the integrating process discussed in Chapter 5, making connections among individual innovators who otherwise would be unlikely to meet or work together. As Julia Hitzbleck, who built up the Ambassador Network, puts it, "Accounting, procurement, sales . . . they all have different needs, but we want them to have a common language." Under the leadership of the I-Coaches, "they build road maps, run innovation workshops, engage their local colleagues, and make sure things are actually happening."[3]

Bayer's twenty-first-century drive to encourage innovation at all levels of the company has featured other activities to promote and publicize creative thinking. These include Innovation Days and coworking events at which new business concepts have been presented at Bayer facilities in locations from Shanghai and Tokyo to Boston and Berlin. But on a day-to-day basis, the work of the I-Coaches has played the biggest role in spreading the culture of innovating into every corner of Bayer.

Every company will design the structure and activities of its I-Team to suit its own corporate culture, needs, and innovation objectives. At Sabancı Holding, for example, Burak Turgut Orhun, head of strategy and business development, has created a system for recruiting employees to become members of what he calls X-teams, which are in charge of leading special high-profile, groupwide innovating projects. Each X-team includes workers from different companies within the group, who are selected with the help of human resources specialists. An X-team is typically assigned one highly promising innovating idea, which it shepherds through a development process known as the Innovation Funnel, a task that normally lasts about three months. Orhun has found that the employees who make the best candidates for X-team roles are those with highly flexible, open-minded attitudes—people he likes to refer to as "misfits" or "pirates." It's a job that has become highly prized within the Sabancı group; in fact, employees who have formerly served as members of an X-team often proudly mention it soon after meeting a new colleague.[4]

In 2019, Fiskars, the Finnish company whose innovating methods we explored in Chapter 5, created a new centralized innovating unit named Bruk (the original name of the village where Fiskars was founded in 1649). "If the R&D team at Fiskars is the innovation hub for physical products," says Tomas Granlund, the leader of Bruk, "then Bruk is the innovation hub for disruptive innovations of other kinds, especially when it comes to digital services and business model innovation."[5] Bruk invites ideas from both external partners and Fiskars' employees in any department. It periodically launches "business challenges" around specific themes such as sustainability with the goal of quickly designing prototypes for testing and further development. In short, Bruk is a specialized I-Team unit built to meet a specific need within Fiskars' innovating engine.

I-Coaches as Trainers and Teachers

At Bayer, the I-Coaches help to train their colleagues in using innovating methods and tools. Since 2016, Bayer has trained more than 1,000 employees in innovation methods such as Systematic Inventive Thinking, Design Thinking, and Lean Startup.

The Lean Startup methodology, associated with the work of Eric Ries, entrepreneur, venture advisor, and author, has proven to be particularly valuable. With its wise mantra of "Fall in love with your problem, not your solution," it encourages continual, open-minded rethinking of any innovative idea. Lean Startup also emphasizes the importance of objective experimentation and testing before any new idea is deemed ready for widespread adoption.

Bayer has taken this philosophy to heart. Dr. Lessl told me about a typical example of how fast prototyping and repeated experiments are being used to test and refine product and service ideas in today's Bayer. One of the important market segments Bayer seeks to serve in India is the vast number of smallholder farmers, who manage tiny plots of land but who raise, in the aggregate, a large percentage of the food that supports this huge, sprawling country. These smallholder farmers, who play such an important role in supporting India's food security, could benefit greatly from the products, tools, and information that Bayer's crop science division could offer them—but bringing these goods to millions of farmers in thousands of remote villages is a huge challenge.

In response, as part of the CATALYST program, a local Bayer team came up with an idea for a chatbot that could connect with Indian farmers through the cell phones that nearly all of them now own. But rather than simply designing such a bot and putting it on the market, the Bayer team wisely chose to start by applying the Lean Startup methodology of repeated testing and experimentation. First they did a series of interviews with smallholder farmers, individually and in groups, to discuss the kinds of services and information they would like to have access to. Based on this input, the Bayer team drew up 10 different proposals for chatbot services, outlining the kinds of contents to be provided and the cost. They presented these options to a cross section of farmers, asking them, "Which of these services would you buy, and why?" They even set up a temporary website where farmers could pick a chatbot option and fill out a registration form to show their interest.

Only after all that preliminary testing did the Bayer team put together a product prototype that embodied all the features the farmers whom they'd studied found most attractive and valuable. When they made the prototype available on WhatsApp and sent a link to 70 farmers for a final test, they discovered that all their previous experimentation had paid off. Not only did their test group react enthusiastically to the prototype, they passed the word about it on to their friends and relations. In response to the 70 offers the Bayer team sent out, they received 150 subscriptions!

Stories like this show how the innovating expertise that Bayer's I-Coaches are disseminating throughout the organization is paying big dividends in the form of great ideas becoming even better through a well-designed development process.

Whenever new ideas begin to surface in Bayer's creation process, various members of the I-Team get involved. I-Coaches encourage their colleagues to write up brief descriptions and analyses of innovative ideas in the form of simple, one-page proposals. When appropriate, the ideas can simply be submitted to the immediate manager of the innovating person or team. But if this doesn't make sense—for example, if the idea requires buy-in from more than one department or division to be implemented—the idea can be separately submitted to a local I-Coordinator. The coordinator's job is to systematically review innovation ideas and provide prompt feedback. If the idea is promising, the local I-Coordinator can select it and move it to the next step in the review and selection process. Thus, the biggest job of I-Coordinators is in connecting and linking the various innovating teams, capabilities, and new ideas scattered around the organization. They are involved in the channeling, filtering, and selecting process by which a local idea moves from an isolated insight about the customer into a new proposed solution.

Bayer's Catalyst Fund—
Building Bigger Innovations

It is easy to see that members of the I-Team at Bayer, from the I-Coaches through the I-Coordinators, are deeply engaged in a wide range of innovating activities, facilitating the creation and dissemination of a constant stream of ideas for improving Bayer practices and products around the world. But their innovating work doesn't stop there. When posts on the WeSolve forum, fast sessions led by I-Coaches, and other innovating activities surface a really big idea with the potential to generate major benefits for Bayer and its customers, another innovating system springs to life. This is Bayer's Catalyst Fund, a corporate intrapreneurship program that shepherds such highly promising ideas through a funding and development process designed to select and foster the best concepts and turn them into practical realities.

The Catalyst Fund was launched in 2017. With the help of the I-Coordinators, 120 challenges with potential to spawn innovative projects were identified. Eventually 28 topics that showed unusual value-creating promise were selected by the I-Team in close collaboration with senior business leaders. They were then addressed by a small cross-disciplinary team, led by a Lean Startup coach, which was committed to rigorous experimentation and iterative testing of the concept, including fast prototyping. These projects received funding totaling €50,000 (equal to about $60,000) and had three months to explore their solution and pitch it to a venture board of senior executives and innovation ambassadors. For 11 projects that presented the most convincing data, further development and testing followed.

Over time, more challenges were channeled through the Catalyst Fund system; the same winnowing process was used to select winners that would be funded for further development.

One way to think about the Catalyst Fund is as the organ that connects Bayer's horizontal innovating engine to its vertical execution engine. The tools used for testing and refining the raw ideas that emerge from the innovators are designed to ensure that only concepts that are ready to be absorbed into the company's everyday operations make the cut.

Dr. Ouelid Ouyeder, who has been running the Catalyst Fund since 2018, says:

> As of 2020, five Catalyst Fund projects have been successfully launched as new Bayer businesses. They range from a disease prevention program for cats and dogs being offered to veterinarians by Bayer's France-based division to a training program for radiology physicians originating in Bayer's Peruvian operation. More pilot projects are in the pipeline, and in years to come more Bayer businesses are likely to emerge as outgrowths of the Catalyst Fund.

"Innovation Is Contagious": Lessons from the Bayer Experience

In recent years, as Bayer's innovating engine has continued to mature, it has also evolved. During 2020, in response to the worldwide COVID-19 epidemic, practically all of the company's innovating activities have migrated online, a pattern we've seen at many other companies as well. Sustainability—defined in both social and environmental terms—has become an increasingly important part of Bayer's innovating program. The factors on which proposed new projects are measured now include, along with the likely financial results and the marketing possibilities, the positive social impacts that could be generated and the environmental costs and benefits to be expected. "In today's world," Dr. Lessl says, "there is no innovation that's not sustainable, and sustainability needs innovation. The two are a natural and perfect fit."

Company leaders have worked to make sure the new focus on innovating is being integrated into Bayer's cultural DNA. Every learning program for Bayer employees now includes innovation as a central topic, and every list of core competencies used to evaluate new hires and current employees includes innovating.

Finally, the responsibility of the board in supporting innovation has expanded, as the role once filled by a single board member has now been handed over to the entire board, operating as the new, formal I-Committee. This helps to ensure that the focus on innovating from the very highest levels of the organization is never lost.

Some of the lessons from the Bayer innovating experience are familiar ones that align closely with the overall themes of this book. For example, Bayer's Dr. Lessl points to the way innovation relies on teamwork and tends to grow from the middle and lower levels of organizations:

> *Innovation is a social activity, and connectivity is an asset.* The image of the lone inventor is alluring, but almost always wrong. Innovation actually happens in teams, in cross-functional workshops, and through the involvement of many. It is also highly contagious. After we introduced the fast session concept, there were some countries where it took off, with fast sessions every week, and everyone wanting to get involved. This happened not because of a central directive, but because of the energy and skills of a few individuals.[6]

Other lessons from Bayer connect specifically with the role of the I-Coaches. The employees who participate most actively in Bayer's innovating activities—the hundreds of I-Coaches and I-Coordinators who train their colleagues in innovating, lead innovating programs and workshops, and help develop innovative ideas into proposals that may turn into new processes, products, or businesses—are formally charged with the responsibility for this work. They are officially encouraged to devote 5 to 10 percent of their time to innovating work, and they earn so-called star points for each innovating task they perform, an incentive system that Bayer's leaders refer to as "gamified." When an I-Coach has earned 500 star points, he or she is designated an "advanced coach." Advanced coaches have the opportunity to experience a new two-day training program at which they get to further improve their innovating skills.

Interestingly, however, Bayer's Dr. Trill warns against incentivizing managers to innovate by measuring "vanity metrics"—for example, the number of innovative ideas that give rise to new business opportunities, or the cost savings or profit measures generated by an improved system. "Innovation is a tool to achieve the strategy of a business, not a purpose in itself; thus, innovation should be the natural way leaders leverage to drive their business," Dr. Trill says. "That is why innovative behavior should be encouraged or requested, but individual results not incentivized." The results may or may not happen, depending on circumstances. What matters is to define an area where the business needs innovation and systematically explore new opportunities through creativity and rapid experimentation to meet the real needs of the customers. If you do this, you'll create ample opportunities for the results to emerge.

Beyond the cohorts of I-Coaches and I-Coordinators, all employees and managers are important in Bayer's innovating ecosystem. On the most basic level, departmental and division leaders must be willing to give permission and empower employees to devote time and energy to innovating activities—even when this means "stealing" resources from their everyday execution work. Since managers are generally appraised and rewarded for the concrete execution results they achieve—sales racked up, products manufactured, customers served—they are tempted to give innovating short shrift.

Dr. Trill admits that this is a big challenge, even at an innovation-centric company like Bayer. To address it, the company has worked hard to make innovating attractive to managers. Making sure every site has at least one local I-Coach is one useful step. I-Coaches can help locally to solve problems, which often provides direct and immediate benefits to the business and thus to the managers. I-Coaches can also help managers to "fail fast" by triggering the most critical experiments first, reducing the resource costs involved in innovating.

Broader corporate support also helps to encourage managers to embrace innovating. The fact that Bayer's top-level executives, especially the members of the I-Committee, go out of their way to publicly recognize and reward departments and divisions that do a good job of innovating helps to win support from the organization. For example, to encourage widespread use of WeSolve, board member Kemal Malik used to sponsor a regular contest in which employees who posted the best challenges on the online forum would be invited to dinner with Bayer's top executives. Understandably, managers also enjoy basking in the reflected glory they receive when their frontline employees are lauded as heroes of innovating.

What's more, increasing numbers of managers are coming to recognize that supporting innovating activities is a powerful way to attract and retain the best employees. People throughout organizations *want* the chance to innovate; when they are denied the opportunity, they are apt to go elsewhere. Dr. Trill tells the story of a local Bayer manager who discouraged one of his team members from getting involved in innovating projects because her daily work was too demanding and important. Within a few months, she had departed for a job at a rival pharmaceutical firm. When stories like this are shared through the grapevine, they spread the lesson that supporting innovating is smart business in the short term as well as the long term.

Perhaps the most important takeaway from the Bayer story is the way a giant multinational corporation with a rich history of achievement has been able to generate a new vibrant culture of innovation by building an innovating engine in parallel to its highly efficient execution engine—and then by finding ways to engage the majority of its workforce in keeping *both* engines humming.

This is not an easy task for any organization because the two engines are so different in their management styles and structures. The execution engine is about control. Because top management needs to maintain strict control over the activities involved in executing the chosen strategy, allocating scarce resources, setting operating targets, and monitoring results, it's inevitable that most companies will create layers of hierarchy and sophisticated control systems that gradually discourage innovating behavior.

In contrast, the innovating engine is less about control and more about delegation, communication, collaboration, transparency, and team-building. It reflects a different managerial attitude that focuses on allowing individual employees with promising ideas to test, develop, and prove the value of those ideas. The innovating engine allows local departments to support individual innovators whose successful ideas may ultimately give rise to separate, self-supporting departmental or divisional units in a positive, long-term cycle of innovation and growth.

The differences between the execution engine and the innovating engine are stark. Yet Bayer has developed ways to train and encourage managers in every division and functional area to understand and value *both* styles of management and apply them when and where appropriate—a subtle, complex, yet vital leadership challenge.

In companies like Bayer that have found a way to make both engines operate efficiently, the differences between the two core engines of the organization, their management philosophies and practices, become increasingly clear to and internalized by everyone over time. When operating in execution mode, employees and managers have tightly defined job descriptions, elaborate planning processes, and control systems that guide resource allocation decisions. When the same people operate in innovating mode, they dedicate a portion of their time to legitimate, protected, and supported innovating activities within the organization that might be of potential value to a customer and to the company.

As Dr. Lessl says, "Innovation is contagious." At Bayer, the beneficial infection of innovating practices is being spread companywide through a network of systems, processes, and connections that turn employees in every division and department into creators of the future.

KEY TAKEAWAYS FROM CHAPTER 9

- Innovating needs to occur throughout the organization. An I-Team—a formal governance and coordination structure dedicated to *legitimizing, advocating, and sponsoring innovating and spreading information, insight, and practices conducive to innovating*—can play a crucial role in making it happen.
- I-Teams can be structured in many ways, but most include a centrally coordinated unit of *I-Trainers who are charged with training I-Coaches and local teams* in the skills needed to generate and develop innovative ideas.
- Most I-Teams also include *I-Coaches embedded across the breadth and depth of the organization*, who help to guide local teams and individuals as they engage in innovating activities.
- *Local I-Coordinators, also embedded in the organization, play an important role* by making connections among innovators throughout the organization and helping to choose the most promising innovative ideas for further development.
- Within the I-Team, an *I-Committee may be responsible* for selecting the best innovative ideas, making investment decisions, and monitoring results to ensure the most promising ideas get the backing they deserve. From the very top of the organization, the I-Committee proactively advocates, promotes, sponsors, and supports innovating activities throughout the organization.

10

PRIMING THE PUMP

A SEVEN-STEP PROCESS FOR CREATING INNOVATIVE IDEAS

Marvel Comics is an iconic American brand that was founded in 1939, during the golden age of superhero comic books. By the 1960s, Marvel Comics—home to Spider-Man, the Incredible Hulk, the Fantastic Four, and the X-Men—had become the leading challenger to DC Comics, creators of Superman, Batman, and Wonder Woman. Marvel was specially loved for its quirky, often troubled superhero characters and the true-to-life emotional problems they experienced: Peter Parker, the insecure teenager with spider-like powers who nonetheless can't get a date with the girl he likes; Bruce Banner, the emotionally reserved scientist who becomes the Incredible Hulk when his temper is triggered; Tony Stark, the millionaire weapons profiteer with a badly damaged heart who shields himself—physically and emotionally—in an armored suit that turns him into Iron Man.

Unfortunately, during the 1990s, Marvel joined many other companies in falling prey to the age of corporate raiders, junk-bond financing, and extravagant debt. By December 1996, Marvel had gone into a tailspin, forcing it to fire most of its workforce and ultimately to file for bankruptcy. Emerging in 1998, Marvel was cash-starved, saddled with costly debt, and reliant on revenues from steadily declining comic book sales for survival. The company's odds looked poor—until a Hollywood agent (and lifelong comics fan) named David Maisel proposed an innovative new strategy featuring movies built around Marvel's most unique attribute: its roster of compelling, relatable characters.

Marvel was no stranger to Hollywood. Like DC Comics, it had entered licensing deals with some of the biggest movie studios, including Sony, Universal, and Twentieth Century Fox—companies with long histories of experience and expertise in creating successful motion pictures. Unfortunately, the track record of Marvel-based movies had been mixed at best. *Men in Black* (1997) had been a big hit for its day, grossing $253 million. But other Marvel pictures, like *Howard the Duck* (1986), *Punisher* (1991), and *Blade* (1998), had fallen far short of expectations.

Named COO of Marvel Studios in 2004, Maisel set to work implementing his vision. Marvel would no longer license out its characters to outside studios. Instead, it began producing its own movies, which would enable the gradual creation of a "Marvel cinematic universe" (MCU), making possible films in which two or more superheroes would appear together. In March 2007, Maisel named Kevin Feige president of production for Marvel Studios. Feige had been involved with producing Marvel movies since 2000, and his intimate knowledge of the Marvel characters and the universe they inhabited would prove to be crucial to the company's reframing.

In the years that followed, Marvel developed a moviemaking style that represented a radical departure from Hollywood norms. Marvel avoided investing in fancy offices, impressive studios, and sky-high salaries for executives or stars. The company installed its headquarter offices over a car dealership and stocked it with old, used office furniture. Marvel recruited marquee names to appear in their pictures only under special circumstances that allowed the company to pay bargain-basement prices. For example, it cast one-time Oscar nominee Robert Downey, Jr., as Iron Man at a time when a public history of drug problems had made the actor persona non grata to executives at other studios. Rather than hiring directors with track records of success in the superhero genre, Marvel hired ones whose success had come in unrelated movie categories. *Iron Man* was directed by Jon Favreau, best known for low-budget indie films with clever dialogue, such as *Swingers, Elf,* and *Zathura: A Space Adventure.* Favreau brought an attitude of playful experimentation to the movie set, so that costar Jeff Bridges described the project as feeling like "a $200 million student film."[1]

Perhaps most important, Marvel Studios built a production system designed to protect and nurture what the fans loved best—the quirky Marvel superheroes. Eliminating layers of middle management gave filmmakers and screenwriters greater freedom to develop complex stories with edgy, potentially controversial twists, since there were fewer executives with veto power. Marvel also created a Creative Committee, including not just company executives but some of Marvel's top comic book editors, to oversee the production of all the company's movies. For the first time, comic-based movies would be shaped by comic book lovers themselves, ensuring the artistic integrity of the characters and their interweaving storylines.

The results have been amazing. The first movie released by the new Marvel Studios, *Iron Man* (2008), was a blockbuster, grossing $585 million worldwide. Since then, the movie industry has been largely dominated by films set in the MCU, including *The Amazing Spider-Man* (2012), which grossed $758 million; *Captain America: Civil War* (2016), at $1.1 billion; *Black Panther* (2018), at $1.3 billion; *Avengers: Infinity War* (2018), at $2.0 billion; and the champion of them all (so far), *Avengers: Endgame*

(2019), at \$2.8 billion.[2] The last-named movie was also the fastest film in history ever to reach the \$2 billion revenue level.[3] Of the top 10 highest-grossing superhero films of all time, 8 are products of Marvel Studios, as are 4 of the top 10 highest-grossing films in *any* category.

Where Do Great Ideas Come From?

Later in this chapter, we'll take a closer look at how Maisel, Feige, and their associates at Marvel Studios developed the innovative strategy that transformed their business from an ailing also-ran into a world-beating powerhouse. With the benefit of hindsight, some of the moves they made—such as building emotionally complicated stories around the quirky personality traits that made Marvel characters popular in the first place—might appear obvious. But creative ideas that become the foundation for wildly successful multi-billion-dollar businesses are never as easy to recognize and implement as they might appear after the fact. If they were, business success would be a much more commonplace commodity. So we can't simply write off Marvel's extraordinary success as based on "obvious" insights. Real insight is almost never obvious.

On rare occasions, the creation of innovative ideas can be fairly straightforward. Sometimes the arc of technological development points clearly toward future developments with obvious potential to create huge new value for customers and the businesses that serve them. By the 2010s, it didn't take a visionary genius to recognize that automobiles freed from dependence on fossil fuels were the logical next step in transportation technology, which is why research and development departments at all the big automakers were hard at work on developing the technology to make such cars economically practical.

In a handful of other cases, customers may be aware of the kinds of new products or services they need and want, and they may even explicitly request them. More often, however, customers have little or no idea as to what they need or want. This was the case for Marvel comics fans in the late 1990s. It's doubtful that any group of comic-book readers or moviegoers would have been able to explain precisely what they wanted from a Marvel movie. At most, they might have been aware of a vague dissatisfaction or boredom with the existing offerings.

When you face a complicated strategic situation like the one Marvel faced, looking for new ideas "in spite of the customer" may require new skills on your part—new ways of thinking about your business that can help you envisage alternatives you otherwise might not consider. Here is where a practical methodology for sparking and focusing creative thinking can play a valuable role. A well-designed process provides a structure for thinking and behaving; it creates a common language for codifying, storing, and sharing data and information; and it offers a checklist of things to do and questions to ask when innovating. A good process can help you innovate effectively, and to do so repeatedly and consistently, as a routine part of your daily operations. The purpose of this chapter is to provide you with such a process.

In 1998, I started practicing Value Innovation under the guidance of W. Chan Kim and Renée Mauborgne. They are colleagues of mine at INSEAD, where they are codirectors of the Blue Ocean Strategy Institute. They are also authors of the classic 2005 book *Blue Ocean Strategy* as well as a valuable sequel that updates their ideas and offers a host of additional illustrative examples.[4] Over the years, I've learned a great deal from both of these brilliant strategy thinkers, and with their support I've coached a number of companies in using Blue Ocean tools specifically to generate innovative ideas.

In the process, I've adapted the most powerful elements of Blue Ocean Strategy thinking and tools. I've also included additional exploration tools and techniques, integrating the suite of methods into a Seven-Step Innovating Process methodology that applies Blue Ocean thinking to the specific challenge of innovating. The resulting system helps innovators restructure their thinking and effortlessly switch from supplier-side to customer-side thinking.

Because many of the tools I favor have their roots in the Blue Ocean Strategy approach invented by Kim and Mauborgne, I strongly recommend that you read one or both of their books if you are interested in fully mastering the business approach they pioneered. The overview of my adopted methodology in this chapter will offer you a capsule version that I hope will suggest the power of using a systematic process to stimulate valuable creative thinking for anyone in almost any kind of business.*

However, as mentioned previously, I am not dogmatic about insisting on the primacy of any one method for generating innovative concepts. Instead, I recognize that there are a number of methodologies that can be useful to companies seeking ways to jump-start their innovating engines. Indeed, smart people have been producing ingenious approaches to creative thinking at least since 1939. That was the year when a groundbreaking advertising executive named James Webb Young published *A Technique for Producing Ideas,* which people are still reading and using to spark their own innovative brainstorms today.

More recent examples of innovating toolkits include the TRIZ methodology, described in Chapter 2, which helped Samsung's management team focus the creativity of its employees on new product ideas. Offshoots of TRIZ that some organizations employ include SIT (Systematic Inventive Thinking) and USIT (Unified Structured Inventive Thinking). Another well-known innovation technique is Design Thinking, successfully practiced by the design and innovation firm IDEO and popularized in books by Thomas Lockwood, Vijar Kumar, and others.[5]

---

* A more detailed explanation of the Seven-Step Innovating Process and its associated tools can be found on the website www.BTIthebook.com.

In my years as a consultant, trainer, and teacher, I've observed companies using many kinds of tools in the process of generating ideas, sometimes combining elements from one approach with techniques borrowed from other theories and thinkers. Sometimes organizations find it useful to shift from one methodology to another as a way of refreshing the imaginations of their employees and stimulating a new burst of outside-the-box thinking. Be aware that most toolkits have an implicit underlying theory or view of the world. Some toolkits, such as Michael Porter's Five Forces Model and the Boston Consulting Group's Product Portfolio Matrix, tend to assume a supplier-side view of the world; others, like the Design Thinking toolkit and the Jobs-To-Be-Done framework associated with the work of Clayton Christensen, assume a customer-side perspective. When you adopt a specific toolkit, you are also implicitly embracing a particular underlying theory of the business—which is an important reality to understand and learn about.

However, if you have a favorite innovation methodology that you have found effective—or if you are working with an outside consultant who advocates an approach you consider relevant and helpful—that's fine.

I offer my own toolkit of Blue Ocean–inspired methods because it is one set of options that my corporate clients, business-school students, and executive participants have found useful. It's particularly useful in helping businesspeople pivot their thinking from a supplier-side view to a customer-side view, thereby stepping from the execution space into the innovating space.

The Built to Innovate (BTI) Seven-Step Innovating Process

The seven-step process I teach to my corporate clients is designed to be *simple, generic, systematic, repeatable, flexible, adaptable, scalable,* and *visible.* It's designed so that anyone can use it to innovate, and it can work across a wide range of industries, business units, products, services, and functions. First designed and used in one of INSEAD's flagship executive education programs in 2004, it has been continuously modified, updated, and improved ever since. It's designed to work best when it is visible to everyone in the organization—for example, appearing on a corporate portal or as part of the standard training and development program offered to incoming employees. If you want the Seven-Step Innovating Process to produce the best results for your organization, make a point of ensuring that everyone hears about it and knows how to use it.

The seven practical steps in the innovating process are depicted in summary form in Figure 10.1. They include:

1. Choosing a subject for innovating
2. Organizing the project team
3. Codifying the supplier-side view of the subject
4. Understanding the customer experience
5. Exploring noncustomer space
6. Selecting and fast-prototyping the best ideas
7. Presenting and selling the best idea

Let me explain what is involved in each of these steps in turn.

Step 1. Choosing a subject for innovating. The first thing you need to begin your innovating journey is a direction, goal, or general objective. This is the subject about which you hope to innovate. It can be a product, service, technology, internal or external process, organizational function, business model, or perhaps something else that you feel is in need of improvement. The only core requirement for the innovating subject is a target customer—someone for whom you are aiming to innovate, whether this person is external to the organization or internal to it. As you'll see, the goal of the innovating process is to improve the customer's experience—which is why it's essential to identify the target customer at the very start of the innovating process.

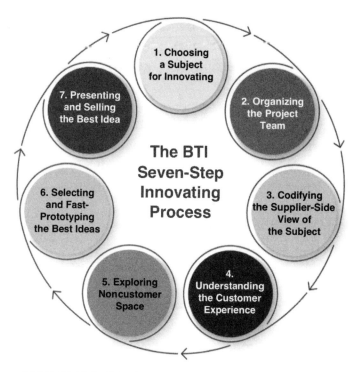

FIGURE 10.1   The BTI Seven-Step Innovating Process

One important caveat, however: Don't allow your choice of a subject to become a straitjacket. The innovating process is a journey of discovery, not a rigid exercise with a preordained conclusion. In the course of your team's work together, it may well happen that you come across one or more additional subjects that are just as ripe for innovating as your initial subject—or more so. Feel free to shift your attention to them. The point is to find ways of creating new forms of value for your organization and for your customers, which frequently involves unplanned detours that lead to unexpected discoveries. Don't reject these discoveries—embrace them!

Step 2. Organizing the project team. The second step in the innovating process is to organize the team of people who will participate in the innovating project. This includes two main tasks: selecting the team members and defining the shared goals, rules, roles, processes, and other requirements the members will need to fulfill.

When it comes to selecting the team members, *diversity* is crucial. This includes diversity in the demographic sense—choosing members of varying ages, genders, ethnic backgrounds, experience levels, and so on. It also includes diversity of thinking, work experience, and views of the business. Subject experts with special knowledge of technology, market dynamics, customer needs, or other topics that could be relevant to the innovating process may need to be brought on board.

People with little or no experience in your industry may also be important to include in the team. Their "naive" questions about deeply ingrained assumptions, norms, and beliefs may play a crucial role in helping the team behave in far more innovative ways than it might otherwise do.

Finally, be sure to include at least a couple of people who will have a role in implementing whatever innovative ideas the team comes up with. These individuals, who may come from departments like operations, production, logistics, and finance, will have critical knowledge of the practical challenges that are likely to arise, and they can help to ensure that the plans your team generates are as realistic as possible.

Once the team members have been identified, you'll need to map out the ways your project team will work together. Take time to discuss and agree on the following preconditions:[6]

- ▶ The shared and collective *goals* that will guide your work
- ▶ The *values* you agree to honor (including, for example, transparency, reliability, and mutual respect)
- ▶ The *rules of engagement* you will follow (regarding such matters as how decisions will be made and how disagreements will be handled)
- ▶ The *roles* individuals agree to take on (such as leader, notetaker, coordinator, and devil's advocate)—all of which may rotate from time to time

▶ The *processes* you intend to use for communication and information-sharing

▶ The *commitments* each team member will make to the group regarding the time, energy, and other resources they will contribute to the team effort

Innovating teams operate differently from most organizational groups. There is no "boss" telling you what to do, nor is there a specific goal preselected by the company leadership. Instead, the team is a self-organizing unit that depends on trust, openness, and mutual support to accomplish anything worthwhile. Discussing basic principles like those listed above will help to ensure that the work of the innovating team is both creative and productive.

Step 3. Codifying the supplier-side view of the subject. The next step in the innovating process is becoming clear about the subject for innovating as you see it today. This means defining the supplier-side view of the subject that members of your organization currently take as they operate the execution engine that dominates their daily work. The goal is to answer the basic questions: Who do we think our customers are? How do we think we are creating value for them and for our organization? For example, if the subject is a product, your supplier-side view will focus on questions like: What do we think are the drivers of willingness to pay for our target customers? How do we think customers feel about our product's quality and its price?

Note that, at this point, your team members are *not* venturing outside of the organization for information to answer these questions. Instead, they are simply defining their own supplier-side view of the issues, based on readily available data. For example, if your subject for innovating is a product, you can refer to sales data, revenue trends, market share statistics, focus group reports, information about quality issues, and more. If your subject is a process or function, you can examine data on inputs and outputs, procedures and controls, cost, capacity, and other information collected from various stages of the activity.

Using all the relevant data and examining what they tell you about key aspects of the subject, jot down notes to capture all of the conclusions you reach. The result will be a written description that captures your present supplier-side mindset or mental model of the subject, based on your beliefs, assumptions, and biases.

Is this view completely accurate? Probably not—its weaknesses and errors will soon be discovered. You'll have an opportunity to engage in some fresh, outside-the-box thinking in the upcoming steps of the Seven-Step Innovating Process. The purpose of step 3 is to first define the contours and size of the current mental box.

Step 4. Understanding the customer experience. Now it's time for the team to pivot from the supplier-side to the customer-side perspective—to step outside the box and begin discovering what the outside world can teach you.

To do this, the innovating project team members must find new sources of information about the customer experience. Going beyond internal reports and analyses, the team members need to step out of the office and the workplace, going out into the field to meet and engage with real customers and other informants who are knowledgeable about the target customer's experience. In-depth conversations should be launched that cover all the stages in the customer journey from the customer's perspective.

If you are a member of such a team, you may find that your study of the customer experience expands to include activities that extend beyond those that are obviously related to your subject. Think, for instance, of the following scenario: a couple with young children goes shopping at a local furniture store. The experience soon turns into a disaster, as the parents have to spend their time chasing the excited little ones around the store to make sure they do not break any lamps and to stop them from jumping on the beds.

Unsurprisingly, the next time the parents need to go furniture shopping, they want to avoid bringing the kids along. But now they have a new problem to solve: Who will take care of the kids? The customer's Job-To-Be-Done now includes finding a family member, friend, or babysitter before that customer can visit the furniture store.

If you were part of an innovating team working for a furniture company, you might not think about this challenge when considering the customer experience. The babysitting problem is not one that furniture customers are likely to mention to anyone from the furniture store they want to visit. Yet the Swedish furniture store chain Ikea recognized this problem—and solved it, by offering supervised on-premises playgrounds for children whose parents are shopping. In a similar fashion, Ikea also added coffee shops and restaurants to its stores, thereby solving other problems that are part of the customer experience (such as the need for nourishment and refreshment during a long day of furniture shopping), even though most customers would never expect a furniture store to address these problems.

How, then, can innovating teams in other industries make sure they discover "the customer's babysitting problem"?

Here is a simple process innovating teams can use to make sure they succeed in hearing both the voice of the customer (the feelings, thoughts, and ideas that customers are expressing more or less openly) and the silence of the customer (the things customers may not be aware of or wouldn't think to share with a supplier). The process includes three steps:

- ▶ The team visually observes and interviews customers as well as other informants who are familiar with the customers' experience and their Job-To-Be-Done. The team members should avoid imposing their own assumptions, beliefs, prejudices, or preferences on the customers. The team members are there simply to ask open-ended questions and to listen and learn actively and empathetically, never lapsing into either the "tell" mode or the "sell" mode.
- ▶ Based on what they see and hear, team members write down what the customers seem to like, dislike, or wish for

during their experience and while trying to accomplish their Job-To-Be-Done. It's critical that these comments are transcribed in the language of the customer rather than being paraphrased or translated into supplier-side jargon.

▶ The collected comments are then organized into categories that make it easy for connecting themes and ideas to emerge.

The best way to organize the comments your team collects is to use what I call a Customer Utility Table (CUT).

A CUT is a table in which the vertical columns represent the various stages of the customer experience—for example, searching for the solution to a problem, choosing from a set of options, buying a product, bringing it home, using it, and so on. The innovating team can create a working list of these stages based on its supplier-side view. Later, as they begin observing and interviewing customers, they can adjust, expand, and improve the list based on the deeper knowledge they are gaining, seeking also to fully capture the stages and activities that happen *before* and *after* the customer interacts with the supplier's product or process.

The horizontal rows in the CUT represent various forms of utility that customers may need or want. I suggest that innovating teams start with the six generic forms of utility as listed by Kim and Mauborgne for the diagram they refer to as a Buyer Utility Map—namely, *Customer Productivity, Simplicity, Convenience, Risk Reduction, Fun,* and *Environmental Friendliness.* The team can modify this list of "utility levers" based on the specific innovating subject and the industry or business context.

When the vertical columns and the horizontal rows are combined, the result is a CUT table that subdivides the universe of the customer experience into a finite number of cells, each representing the intersection of one stage in the customer experience with a particular utility lever. This makes it easier for members of an innovating team to interrogate that entire universe in search of possible places to create new and better ways of creating value. The CUT table offers a simple way of organizing the comments gathered during the visual exploration process. As team members go out into the field and bring back notes based on what they hear and see, the CUT gets filled up with comments, each assigned to an appropriate cell in the table.

I suggest that teams use sticky notes for each comment they collect, color-coded to represent different types of comments: blue for things customers like, red for things customers dislike, and green for things customers wish for. Later, it may be convenient to record them in a printed table or spreadsheet in which the comments are captured and organized by cells.

The evolving CUT, filled with comments in all three colors, constitutes a simple, intuitive, scalable, and fine-grained visualization of what the customer experiences while trying to accomplish the Job-To-Be-Done—all expressed in the customer language and from the customer point of view. As more comments are added, the CUT continues to grow and change. Its appearance helps the team members identify which cells they want to explore more fully during the next round of observations and interviews; cells with few or no comments are those that may demand fuller investigation.

Here's a metaphor that can help you understand the value that a CUT brings to the members of an innovating team. Imagine that a precious diamond has been hidden somewhere in an open field—a field that is covered with long, uncut grasses and tangled weeds. A team of individuals has been given the opportunity to find the diamond. If they discover it within a specified period of time (say, one hour), they can keep it and share its value.

What's the best way for the team members to maximize the chance that they'll find the diamond? The answer: to use a grid to divide the field into a number of distinct sections, each relatively limited in size—then assign team members to scour each of those sections. This method will ensure that no corner of the field goes unexamined.

The CUT table plays the same role for the members of an innovating team. By dividing the space for exploration into distinct, smaller units, it greatly increases the chances that the precious diamond of a brilliant innovating idea will be discovered—no matter where in the customer experience space it may be hidden.

Turning the comments collected in the CUT table into possible innovating ideas is a fairly straightforward process. A blue comment that reflects something customers like can suggest ideas about how to increase, enhance, or expand on that source of value. A red comment that describes something customers dislike can suggest ideas about how to fix the problem. And a green comment that names something customers wish for can suggest ideas about how to satisfy that wish.

It's hard to overstate the value that in-depth observation and interviewing of customers can have for teams trying to generate useful innovating ideas. Let's recall a couple of real-life examples to show how this works.

One is the story from Chapter 6 of the Starwood managers who spent a day roaming the neighborhoods of Paris in search of inspiration for new ideas they could use to revitalize their hospitality business. It was during such a visual exploration that an innovating team from Sheraton Hotels came up with the idea of selling hotel beds as a business. You probably won't be lucky enough to take your innovating team on a trip to the beautiful French capital! But practically everyone can have access to environments that are equally stimulating where it is possible to observe customers in their usual settings and thereby get access to reactions and comments that might otherwise never be observed.

A second example comes from the story of Kordsa, the Turkey-based manufacturer of reinforcing materials. As mentioned in Chapter 4, Kordsa has sent innovating teams into the factories operated by their corporate customers, literally camping out for days at a time to observe what is happening and to talk with employees about what they see. At one tire plant, they noticed that workers were struggling to safely handle rolls of reinforcing fabric that had been loaded onto trucks. The innovating team members realized they were glimpsing a customer problem that Kordsa had never been aware of. Kordsa was subsequently able to remedy the problem by developing a simple, improved method for handling the rolls of fabric and training their customers to use it, reducing the resources needed from 90 minutes and three employees to 12 minutes and a single worker.

Step 5. Exploring noncustomer space. In step 4, the innovating team pivoted from the supplier-side view to the customer-side view. Now in step 5, it's time for them to think even further outside the box, exploring noncustomer space in search of other innovating possibilities. The Six Paths Analysis, a tool derived from the Blue Ocean Strategy approach, offers a specific tool for doing this. It lists six new directions for development that your company can consider to break away from its current framing:

▸ *Path 1: Across Alternative Industries or Solutions.* Let's define the existing customer space along the two dimensions of the target customer and the specific Job-To-Be-Done by the target customer. The resulting noncustomer space, then, includes any space outside your organization's current boundaries on either of these two dimensions. Fiskars, for example, stayed focused on its target customer (home gardeners), but explored what other Jobs-To-Be-Done it could help with. That's how Fiskars decided to enter a new industry—the watering and irrigation business.

▸ *Path 2: Across Customer Groups or Segments.* In other cases, companies seek out new sets of customers they can serve with the same Job-To-Be Done. For example, Nintendo built a successful business around its block-buster Game Boy video system, which targeted boys as

well as solitary and hardcore gamers—a significant segment of the gaming universe, but one that left out many
other potential customers. In time, Nintendo found innovative ways to expand its market—first by creating a new
Game Boy version designed to appeal to girls, then by
launching the Wii game system, which targets occasional
gamers, groups of friends and family members playing
together, and even elderly patients in nursing homes.

▶ *Path 3: Across Actors in the Company's Business Ecosystem.*
A company's ecosystem includes not just the target customers but an entire network of organizations involved
in the delivery of the product or service to the customer,
from suppliers and intermediaries to influencers, prescrib-
ers, regulators, complementors, and government agencies.
Sometimes a company can find ways to create new value
for customers by working with one or more organizations
in this ecosystem. Remember, for example, how Recruit's
CarSensor division—a business-to-consumer media business that provided information about used cars—created
a whole new business by creating a business-to-business
platform that matches upstream companies with supplies
of used cars with downstream companies that need to
purchase such cars.

▶ *Path 4: Beyond the Scope of Activities in the Customer
Experience.* The columns in the CUT table delineate
the scope of activities in the customer experience. Yet as
we've seen, observation and interviews will help to reveal
activities that precede or follow the customer's direct
engagement with the company's product or process. Ikea,
for instance, created new value for customers by solving
a problem they faced even before going to the furniture store.

▶ *Path 5: Across Sources of Appeal, Functional or Emotional.*
The CUT table can help the innovating team determine
how they are trying to appeal to the target customer. The

collected comments in the table may reveal a dominant focus on either functional appeal or emotional appeal—in which case the team may choose to explore the *opposite* source of appeal or a *different type* of functionality or emotion. Ecocem, for instance, took advantage of an underused technological innovation—ground granulated blast furnace slag (GGBS), with a much smaller carbon footprint than conventional cement—and used it to add the emotional appeal of environmental friendliness to the traditional functional appeal its products offered.

▶ *Path 6: Across Time and Trends (the "Back to the Future" Analysis).* An innovating team can explore noncustomer space by imaginatively stepping into the DeLorean time machine and traveling 3, 5, or 10 years into the future. What trends or changes—environmental, technological, political, cultural, social, economic, or demographic—have changed the customer's world? After examining these forces, the team can return to the present and consider ways of anticipating and responding to those trends. An innovating team I coached from a bank in the United Arab Emirates worked backward from the future needs of the children of its wealthy clients. To create value for these future customers and win their loyalty, the team members proposed to organize college tours to prestigious US universities, help the students prepare their college applications, and even arrange a group trip to an international soccer match for them to enjoy.

The Six Paths Analysis in step 5 is a great way to develop innovating ideas to complement those generated during step 4.

Step 6: Selecting and fast-prototyping the best ideas. You now have a huge collection of innovating ideas, generated by your immersive study of customers and of the noncustomer space. Now it's time to select the best of these ideas for possible implementation.

First, the team needs to take a step back, review all the ideas it has generated, and cluster them together. Similar ideas—those that seem to be connected or interdependent—can be aggregated under one cluster, for which the team creates a catchy tag line. The one or a handful of these clusters must be chosen to present to senior management for possible further development. Sometimes the team can easily choose the best idea; in other cases, it's harder to identify the most promising option. To facilitate this decision, the team can rate the idea clusters on three dimensions:

- ▸ The potential value created by the idea for the customer and for the company (i.e., the Value Test from chapter 2)
- ▸ The idea's potential strategic impact
- ▸ The idea's likely ease of implementation

The ideas that rate best according to the combined impact of these three factors will be the ones that move to the next phase, which I refer to as fast prototyping. It's a process that helps to "crash test" and roughly validate the potential for success of the team's top ideas. As Tom and David Kelley of IDEO explain, "The reason for prototyping is experimentation—the act of creating forces you to ask questions and make choices. It also gives you something you can show to and talk about with other people."[7] Many preliminary prototypes fail, which is actually a good thing—when an idea's weaknesses are revealed early, it prevents the waste of time and money as well as potential embarrassment in front of senior leaders.

Creating prototypes for the best idea clusters need not be an elaborate process. It can be as simple as developing a storyboard, poster, group role-playing skit, or homemade gadget to illustrate how the idea might work in real life. The prototype should not be designed to look pretty but simply to highlight the distinctive value the new idea might create for the customer.

Step 7. Presenting and selling the best idea. In many organizations, the Seven-Step Innovating Process is carried out in parallel by a number of teams from various business departments or functions. The result is a big assortment of innovating ideas that could be implemented, from which the organization's senior management must choose one or a few winners. One very effective method for carrying out the selection process culminates in an activity known as a Visual Fair.

The Visual Fair is a kind of "beauty contest" that enables one or more winning ideas to be selected from among those generated by the project teams. On an appointed day, using a simple, standard format, each team presents its top ideas to a select panel that might include executive committee members, senior business unit leaders, relevant midlevel coaches, and I-Team members. The presentations should focus on just a few key points: the nature of the new idea, briefly described; the new value created for the target customers; the new value created for the company; the sources of the idea (including, for example, quotes or insights gathered during the CUT and the Six Paths Analysis). It's very helpful to have a standard presentation format that everyone knows about within the organization.

After a series of short, focused presentations, the Visual Fair may move to a gallery walk, where images and texts depicting the new ideas are displayed for everyone to study. Snacks and beverages may be served, creating a festive atmosphere and a mood of anticipation. After the panelists have had a chance to confer privately, they announce the winners for this Visual Fair—a set of ideas that will be handed over to the execution engine for final testing and implementation by the organization.

Ways of Using the Seven-Step Innovating Process

The Seven-Step Innovating Process is designed to be easily replicable. Many organizations like to conduct the process on a regular basis—once or twice a year, for example. The result is a regular stream of innovating ideas that can become the source of significant new value for both the company and its customers. Some organizations make the CUT tables developed by their innovating teams available on a digital platform, creating an extraordinary device for organizational learning and a rich knowledge base concerning the customer experience. Even more important, employees gradually internalize the activities of the innovating process as well as its underlying principles. Innovating becomes second nature throughout the organization, even when the formal process itself may not be under way.

The flexibility of the Seven-Step Innovating Process means it can be used for a variety of purposes. For example, there are times when an entire organization is badly in need of a strong dose of innovation. Technological changes, marketplace shifts, aggressive moves by disruptors, or sheer inertia may have left an organization at a competitive disadvantage. When this happens, the senior leadership team may choose to put together an innovating team to help look for an entirely new market space, disruptive blockbuster product, or new business model for the organization. The seven-step process can work effectively for this purpose. You might compare this use of the process to a team of athletes competing in the Olympic Games—a major effort with ambitious, world-class-level goals.

Alternatively, a midlevel coach in any department of an organization can choose to implement the seven-step process whenever it seems useful to jump-start the innovating spirit. In this case, the process can be tailored to pursue less lofty though still important goals, such as finding ways to improve a specific product, to enhance customer service, or to streamline one or more internal activities. The process can also be used within a company department on a regular basis—once a year, for example—to identify a range of opportunities for innovating.

This use of the process could be compared to the daily or weekly exercise routine that a health-conscious person follows to stay fit and develop muscle mass. When employees use the seven-step process repeatedly, they find that their "innovating muscles" become strengthened. Ideas for improving the business seem to pop up routinely, and the path to developing and implementing them seems easier and more natural than ever before. This is a fundamental benefit of using the Seven-Step Innovating Process as part of your company's regular behavior, thereby embedding innovating into your organizational DNA.

The Reframing of Marvel Studios as Seen Through the Seven-Step Innovating Process

The Seven-Step Innovating Process can be a powerful way to inculcate innovating behavior throughout an organization. The examples I've mentioned from the experience of companies like Ikea, Starwood, Ecocem, Fiskars, Kordsa, Recruit, and Nintendo illustrate how it happens. But the ideas underlying the seven-step process and its associated tools can also generate valuable innovations even when the formal process is not explicitly used.

To show you what I mean, let's see how some of the innovative tools from the seven-step process can illuminate the steps that Maisel and Feige used to jump-start innovation at Marvel Studios.[8]

First, the Marvel Studios team created superior value for its target customer and for the company by making a series of decisions about ways to bring greater perceived value to moviegoers—all growing from the core strategy of building pictures around the uniquely human qualities of the Marvel superheroes. Team members focused on emotion-laden storytelling, since this was at the heart of the Marvel comics appeal. They built a process, including the Marvel Creative Committee, to safeguard the integrity of the Marvel characters from one film to the next, to ensure that fans will never feel betrayed by a discordant scene or characterization in a Marvel movie.

At the same time, they made critical decisions to reduce their cost structure. No more fancy production offices and no need for redundant layers of middle management oversight, which would add nothing to the richness of the story lines or the uniqueness of the Marvel characters—and, in fact, might simply discourage the creativity of the Marvel moviemakers by increasing the level of financial risk they faced. The team also chose not to rely on overly expensive proven box-office talent, since the superheroes themselves, not expensive marquee names, would be the real attraction to audiences.

In all these ways, the Marvel team members responded to what they learned by studying their existing customers and making choices that improved the level of value created for those customers.

The Six Paths Analysis further illuminates the creative thinking behind Marvel's success. Marvel Studios broke the mold of traditional superhero filmmaking by leveraging two paths to market from step 5 that other studios had neglected. Team members journeyed *across customer segments* by developing movies that appealed to a much broader array of customers than the adolescent comic-book fans, mostly male, who constitute the core audience for traditional superhero movies. The team achieved this, in large part, by shifting *across functional and emotional appeals*. Rather than relying mainly on the forms of value delivered by most superhero films—plenty of high-speed, often violent action and eye-popping special effects—team members crafted stories that included complex character arcs, subtle emotional conflicts, and political and social overtones.

Because Marvel chose these two paths from the Six Paths Analysis, movie lovers who don't usually care for comic-book stories, including women and older adults, found themselves drawn to the Marvel films. Even the critics and movie industry gatekeepers have been impressed. Marvel's movies have earned an impressive average approval rating on the Rotten Tomatoes website of 84 percent, and they've garnered an average of 64 award nominations apiece.[9] Marvel Studios has managed to open up a new market space for superhero movies, reaching viewers that other studios creating films in the same genre have only been able to dream about.

Continuing to Innovate: Marvel's Future

At the end of 2009, Marvel was acquired for $4.2 billion by Disney. At the time, the reframing of Marvel Studios' movie business had just begun. But the transfer of ownership didn't derail the process. Since its founding in 1923, the Walt Disney Company has been famous for its unique brand of commercially successful entertainment innovation. It seems clear that it recognized the fact that the newly minted Marvel Studios team was developing a formula of its own that could deliver blockbuster hits with remarkable regularity.

In this respect, the Marvel acquisition strongly resembles another Disney purchase, that of Pixar Animation Studios in 2006. Pixar is perhaps the only other movie studio of recent years with a track record of innovation comparable to Marvel's. As of 2021, Disney is deploying both of these formidable assets— along with its ownership of such other prized franchises as the Star Wars saga and, of course, its own storied catalog of animated classics—to enable its new streaming service, Disney+, to compete against the likes of Netflix and Amazon.

Meanwhile, Marvel Studios has become a mainstay of its parent company's financial success. In 2019, Marvel's biggest hit, *Avengers: Endgame,* generated fully 15 percent of Disney's total revenues of $69 billion.[10] And Marvel Studios president Feige is promising more hits that offer a continuing stream of creative innovations. "We've got another 20 movies on the docket," he has boasted, "that are completely different from anything that's come before—intentionally."[11]

Still, consistently cranking out Hollywood hits, even according to a proven formula, is far from easy. A group of business experts who analyzed how it works described the reality this way: "Just making a movie successful enough to support a franchise is hard: Six of the eight *worst-performing* big-budget films in 2017 were meant to start new franchises" (emphasis added). They went on to quote no less an expert than Jon Favreau, director of Marvel's own *Iron Man,* on the elusiveness of long-term success for action movie franchises. "It's very difficult to keep these franchises from running out of gas after two [movies]," Favreau said. "The high point seems to be the second one, judging by history."[12] With 23 movies from the Marvel universe so far, one could be forgiven for thinking that this franchise might be running on borrowed time.

The time will surely come—sooner or later—when Marvel Studios finds that its brilliant formula for movie success is beginning to run out of steam. When that happens, the leadership team will need to consider yet another innovative reframing. They may choose to use an innovation methodology like the one presented in this chapter. Such a systematic process can make it easier for any team of employees at any organization to begin generating, vetting, and perfecting valuable new ideas to fuel the innovating engine.

KEY TAKEAWAYS FROM CHAPTER 10

- A systematic approach to innovating can help teams at every level of an organization learn and master *insightful, customer-centered ways of thinking.*
- The Seven-Step Innovating Process and the associated tools described in this chapter can help you choose subjects for innovation, pivot from the supplier-side to the customer-side view of your business, explore the noncustomer space, and consider alternative paths for expanding your value-creating activities.
- They can also help you generate innovative ideas, select the best ideas for development, and define a competitive strategy that will differentiate your company from your rivals, enabling you to offer *unique value* to a large, loyal, and growing set of customers.
- The Seven-Step Innovating Process can help your organization meet a major competitive challenge. It can also be used as a routine practice to produce a steady stream of small but valuable innovations. When you use the process this way, *the "innovating muscle" of your entire organization is strengthened.*

11

KEEPING THE ENGINE HUMMING

NURTURING THE HABIT OF INNOVATING

When a big, ambitious company is floundering, executives are often tempted to "go big" with innovation. They may choose to bet the company on a visionary moonshot-style program, perhaps one developed by a handful of technical wizards in a secret skunkworks isolated from the rest of the business, with the goal of creating a breathtaking new product or service that blows away the competition.

It's a glamorous, exciting strategy—and occasionally it even works.

But history shows that, more often, companies that bounce back from near-death experiences do so not through a single "big bang" of creativity. A much better strategy is making innovating a habit that permeates the organization, generating dozens of small improvements that ultimately add up to a giant turnaround.

That's the path chosen in 2010 by J. Patrick Doyle, then CEO of Domino's Pizza, and the team that surrounded him. At that moment, the company was in trouble. Not only was Domino's a dismal second to its archrival Pizza Hut in revenues, profits, and market share—and slipping further—but its reputation among pizza lovers was crummy. As one company executive ruefully recalls, customers viewed Domino's as "fast food" and "cheap food"—but never as "good food."[1]

Today, a little more than a decade later, all of that has changed.

Domino's journey from worst to first began with a dramatic public commitment by the company's top leaders. In 2010, they launched an ad campaign that confessed to consumers that Domino's pizza had been subpar. The ads even included actual footage from focus groups showing customers saying that Domino's crust "tastes like cardboard" and calling the product "the worst excuse for pizza I've ever eaten." Having eaten a plateful of crow, the company then introduced a new recipe that improved the flavor and texture of the company's crust, sauce, toppings, and cheese.

This act of radical honesty not only captured the attention of customers; it also sent a signal to every Domino's employee. In the words of Dennis Maloney, the company's chief digital officer, "From that point forward, a couple of things started to change. . . . One, I think we became a much more honest and transparent brand both to our customers and internally. Two, we started asking ourselves: Is what we're working on something that would make our customers stop and say, 'Did Domino's really just do that?'"[2]

In other words, the ad officially signaled the launch at Domino's of an era of innovation.

In this chapter, I'll look at the Domino's saga of innovating, reframing, and reinvention. Along the way, we'll tease out a series of lessons that other companies can learn from what the pizza masters did. Domino's story shows how a company that's facing tough competition in a mature industry can transform its fortunes by pulling together all the elements needed to make its everyday innovating engine run at full speed and peak efficiency—not just in the C-suite but at every level and in every department of the organization.

How Domino's Put Innovating at the Heart of Its DNA

Domino's groundbreaking 2010 ad campaign, which introduced its improved pizza recipe under the cheeky tagline "Oh Yes We Did," was only the first step in a lengthy campaign to transform the business. In the years since then, Domino's has followed up with a stream of customer-centered innovations, developed not by outside consultants or a centralized team of experts but by frontline innovators and midlevel coaches in departments across the company.

Realizing that a whole-of-company effort was needed to lift Domino's out of its business doldrums, the organization's leadership proselytized about the importance of cross-company collaboration. This led to the forging of some unlikely internal alliances. For example, when company leaders realized that one of the central arenas for service improvement would be the use of digital technology to make pizza deliveries faster and easier, they mandated regular biweekly working sessions between the IT and marketing departments. Their goal was to avoid the common problem of cool-sounding tech innovations that actually provide little or no value for customers.

It worked. Domino's marketing team mined its insights into customer behavior and preferences to begin generating a stream of ideas for new services that could be implemented through digital technologies. The IT people appreciated the opportunity to learn exactly how their work would impact Domino's customers and to participate in the creative process alongside their colleagues, rather than simply being handed a coding assignment to execute. The result was an unusual partnership. As CDO Maloney explains, "The connection between our IT organization and the marketing organization is probably the best relationship between any two groups in the entire company, which is a really unusual thing to say. . . . Our organization's structure ensures these two groups are working completely in lockstep."[3]

This partnership helped generate a remarkable series of innovative moves, many of them technology-based, that would shake up the pizza industry. They included:

▶ The first pizza-buying app that let customer monitor the progress of their order (2010)
▶ The first voice-activated pizza delivery assistant, an app nicknamed "Dom" (2013)
▶ The first Twitter-based pizza-ordering system (2015)
▶ The first fleet of purpose-built pizza-delivery cars with warming stations designed to keep up to 80 pizzas hot and fresh (2015)
▶ The first experimental pizza-delivery drone (2016)
▶ The first experiments (partnering with Ford) in the use of autonomous, driverless vehicles for pizza deliveries (2018)
▶ The first "geo-fencing" program for digital food ordering, which empowers pizza delivery to over 200,000 outdoor locations (such as local parks) without the need for a street address (2018)
▶ The first GPS tracking system to let customers and store managers map the progress of a pizza delivery in real time (2019)

The 2010s were an era when large swathes of business were being transformed by digital technologies. But few companies—especially in traditional low-tech industries like food service—were as aggressive in pursuing digital innovation as Domino's. By 2019, more than half of Domino's 1,000 corporate employees were working in IT, and the digital reframing of the company was having a major impact on the company's daily operations.[4] Hungry customers could order a Domino's pizza via any device—computer, phone, smartwatch, tablet, digital assistant, even a Samsung TV remote—using clicks, characters, Tweets, Facebook messages, or voice commands. Domino's trumpeted this versatility in another ad campaign, this one with the hashtag #AnyWare.

Today, 75 percent of the pizza orders processed by Domino's are online orders, half of those through mobile devices. Compare this figure with the 5 to 10 percent at the average quick-service restaurant. Domino's has also continually refined and streamlined the available array of ordering methods, steadily reducing the layers of friction that discourage customers from completing an e-commerce transaction. The ultimate solution (as of 2021): "zero-click ordering," in which the customer merely has to open the Domino's app. The software remembers their favorite pizza style and submits an order for it after a 10-second confirmation countdown.[5]

No wonder Domino's likes to describe itself as an e-commerce company—or even "a technology company that delivers pizza."[6]

Not all of Domino's innovations are tech-based. Remember that the company's entire saga of reinvention began with a new pizza recipe designed to simply make the core product more delicious. Domino's continually strives to improve on those kinds of food-service basics. For example, its most recent wave of store openings in the United States focuses on upscale neighborhoods rather than the traditional strip malls, and its newest franchisees are being encouraged to install open kitchens to promote an image of fresh, wholesome food preparation.[7] And while Domino's deliberately avoids the practice of constantly cycling new items onto its menu as some other fast-food chains do, it selectively announces carefully pretested new products that it believes will stand the test of time—most recently, the new

Chicken Taco Pizza and Cheeseburger Pizza options introduced in August 2020.

Thus, while Domino's loves how digital technology can improve its customer service, it also respects the fundamental value of delicious, well-prepared food. Every corporate employee, including those at the C-suite level, learn the traditional basics of pizza-making at Pizza Prep School, and company chief Richard E. Allison, Jr. vows, "As long as I'm the CEO here, we will always make our pizzas by hand."[8]

Creative ideas from frontline innovators who are not working at Domino's headquarters are also welcomed and embraced. Some of these emanate from the franchise owners who operate the thousands of restaurants around the United States and the world. For example, one franchisee in the Seattle area came up with the idea of providing electric bikes to their delivery workers—a faster, safer, and greener alternative to cars or manual bikes. Now electric bikes are being offered to franchisees across the country.[9]

Over the past decade, each of the company's cascading series of innovations garnered headlines for Domino's and captured the attention of the public as well as of Domino's thousands of employees around the world. The company does a great job of spreading the word about its latest big ideas through mainstream media as well as industry-specific channels. For this reason, you might be tempted to dismiss some of these breakthroughs as mere "publicity stunts" rather than being genuinely customer-driven.

However, the evidence strongly suggests that Domino's innovations have actually made the company's products significantly more attractive to pizza lovers. Individual consumers personally validate the fact that Domino's innovations were not just cool ideas cooked up by some nerd who never wondered whether pizza lovers would give a darn. Instead, they actually made the process of getting a pizza easier, faster, and more fun. Customer Laura Khalil, speaking with a reporter for the *Detroit Free Press,* expressed the feelings of many other pizza lovers when she said of Domino's, "They understand people's desire to have things when they want it, how they want it—and get it through the channels they use. It's genius."[10]

Because Domino's innovations generate real (rather than illusory) customer value, it makes good sense for the company to publicize them as widely as possible. The free media that they attract supplements Domino's extensive paid advertising, generating buzz among customers and curiosity among those who haven't already tried Domino's products. It also boosts morale among franchisees and employees, reminding them that Domino's is not just "any old fast-food place" but a center of creative excellence, one of *Fast Company* magazine's most innovative companies in the world.[11]

When it's truly deserved, a widely known reputation for innovation is a powerful way to attract even more creative talent and to encourage your people to keep the innovating engine humming.

"Excellence Is a Habit": Continuous Innovating in Good Times and Bad

No single innovation among the many that Domino's has pioneered during the past decade was revolutionary all by itself. But their combined impact has been remarkable. Thanks to Domino's steady stream of small, impactful innovations, the company doubled its market share, from 9 to 18 percent, within eight years. In the process, it became the world's fastest-growing quick-service restaurant business. And in early 2018, Domino's fulfilled CEO Doyle's long-time dream of passing Pizza Hut as the world's biggest pizza company, with annual sales in excess of $12 billion. (Just a few months thereafter, Doyle passed the baton to Richard Allison.) Today, Domino's boasts more than 16,000 locations, almost 6,000 of them in the United States, the rest in 80 countries around the world.

The company is not resting on its innovative laurels. Instead, it is positioning itself to develop even more new ways to serve customers better in the years to come. In August 2019, Domino's opened an Innovation Garage at its headquarters in Ann Arbor, Michigan—a 33,000-square-foot facility where new in-store and delivery technologies are being developed and tested. There's room for up to 150 employees to work on projects like Domino's R2 rover, an autonomous pizza-delivery device being developed by the robotics company Nuro.[12]

When a business makes innovating an anyone, anytime, anywhere activity, the way Domino's Pizza has done, breakthrough performance in many forms becomes more likely. Domino's embraced this notion of modest but continual innovation quite deliberately. Maloney explains it like this: "We don't want people to think about [innovation] projects as long or drawn-out processes. . . . You have to think about [breaking] things into really small, fast-evolving steps and processes."[13] In other words, don't worry about moon shots; instead, do a lot of good little things as quickly and well as you can. The cumulative result is that the stream of innovations becomes even more powerful.

Companies in every industry would do well to emulate Domino's embrace of continuous innovating. Innovating should become a habit, an activity everyone engages in on a periodic, regular basis as part of a natural routine, just as health-conscious people incorporate an exercise routine into their daily lives. Innovating is a process, not a result. Over time, the constant practice of innovating generates a kind of muscle memory by which the habit of innovating becomes continuous and instinctual rather than relying on random bursts of creativity.

Many organizations feel the sudden urge to jump-start their innovating engine in times of crisis—when profits have dwindled, costs are out of control, customers are complaining about quality, or competitors have seized market share. But the most effective leaders don't wait for a panic situation to flex the company's innovating muscle. Instead, they make sure that all employees train their innovating muscles on a regular basis. Each employee, for instance, should participate in a regular routine of exercises that involve talking with customers (and noncustomers) and sharing their findings with colleagues. The Seven-Step Innovating Process presented in Chapter 10 offers a practical vehicle for organizing activities like these.

When the habit of innovating has permeated an organization, its people find methods to improve their operations every day, in ways big and small, even when everything is going smoothly and the business seems to have no urgent need for reframing. At the same time, they are also ready to respond quickly and creatively when a crisis does hit.

In 2020, restaurants everywhere—including fast-food servers like Domino's—were devastated by the onset of the COVID-19 pandemic. In cities, states, and countries around the world, complete lockdowns or severe restrictions were imposed on public eateries, often with little advance notice and according to unpredictable, seemingly arbitrary protocols. Thousands of restaurants went out of business; thousands more struggled to survive. Two of Domino's major competitors—California Pizza Kitchen and NPC International, the parent company of Pizza Hut—were forced to file for bankruptcy.

Domino's was a huge exception to this pattern. Its decade-long campaign of innovation had already prepared it to respond to the bewildering new demands of customers who could no longer order and enjoy pizza with the freedom and flexibility they were accustomed to. Because Domino's had developed 15 different ways to let people order its products, it was ready to serve customers no matter which channel they gravitated to in the strange new world of COVID.

The company was also primed to deliver new innovations in response to the specific challenges created by the pandemic. For example, to facilitate and enhance the new practice of "contactless delivery" that COVID-shy customers demanded, frontline innovators at many of Domino's 6,000 US locations began offering carside delivery, which allowed customers to receive their pizzas without leaving their vehicles. To make contactless home deliveries more palatable, one frontline innovator fashioned a cardboard Pizza Pedestal to hold the box containing a hot pizza off the ground. (Customers hate finding their pizza box lying on the front step like a discarded newspaper.) The Domino's driver can display the pizza in this way while remaining six feet away when the customer emerges from the front door to accept the delivery. Within weeks, pizza pedestals were in use by Domino's stores around the country.

The pandemic also highlighted another, more subtle benefit derived from Domino's commitment to continuous innovating. Back in 2015, third-party food-delivery businesses like Grubhub and DoorDash had begun to emerge, offering their services to restaurants that didn't have the resources to build their own delivery systems. Domino's competitors like Pizza Hut and Papa John's started making use of these third-party services—but Domino's had no need to do so because it was able to deliver its products more quickly and profitably than any third-party operation could have done. This remained true even when the pandemic exerted additional stress on food-delivery systems. Providing its own delivery services enabled Domino's to retain control of all the information generated by the chain's estimated 85 million active customers as well as the 23 million members of its loyalty program.

CEO Allison says, "We have a tremendous customer base data set. I just can't understand why I'd want to give that to a competitor."[14] Because Domino's innovation has kept it several steps ahead of the market, the company remains in control of its information—which helps it remain in control of its destiny.

In all these ways, the flexibility and creativity that Domino's people developed through years of continuous innovating have paid off. During the pandemic, the company's business has boomed, even as patterns of consumption have shifted. While weekend and late-night pizza orders dwindled—partly because of the decline in parties and gatherings organized around big sporting events—lunch and dinner orders from families stuck at home exploded. Average order sizes also grew, as homebound people weary of cooking bought extra pizza and other items to stock their refrigerators.

Company data reflected these positive trends. During the first quarter of 2020, even as a worldwide recession hit, Domino's global sales actually increased by 4.4 percent, and US same-store sales grew by 1.6 percent as compared with the previous year. (That marked Domino's thirty-sixth consecutive quarter of same-store sales growth in the United States.[15]) By June 2020, three months into the pandemic, Domino's reported that it was hoping to recruit up to 10,000 more delivery drivers—this at a time when other food-service companies were shutting their doors, contributing to a massive worldwide unemployment problem.[16]

●—●—●

The Greek philosopher Aristotle wrote, "We are what we repeatedly do. Excellence, therefore, is not an act, but a habit." As the Domino's story vividly illustrates, the same is true of innovating. It, too, must become a habit rather than a mere act. When your entire organization plays a role in keeping the innovating engine humming, then innovating becomes an everyday activity—one that can help to ensure that your company remains ahead of the curve in a rapidly changing world.

KEY TAKEAWAYS FROM CHAPTER 11

- Many successful companies undervalue the need for innovating until a competitive crisis strikes. Instead, *make innovating a habit,* which can help you remain several steps ahead of the competition.
- Big, market-moving innovations are rare, but *a continual stream of small, incremental innovations* can have an even greater cumulative impact.
- If you simply commit to *regularly spending time and energy on the practice of innovating,* your chances of becoming one of the most innovative organizations in your industry— as well as one of its most successful—will skyrocket.

APPENDIX

	Frontline Innovators	Midlevel Coaches	Senior Leaders
Reframing	· Look for new, nontraditional sources of ideas (e.g. in non-customer space) · Explore broader ecosystem and build new relationships	· Give frontline innovators permission to innovate · Build a sense of trust and safety by embedding fair process	· Create overarching corporate purpose and future ambition · Challenge embedded beliefs and assumptions about customers and the organization · Put innovation at the core of corporate strategy
Integration	· Participate in innovating · Manage and expand own innovating social network · Codify customer observations · Help to build shared knowledge base · Coach other frontline innovators	· Link ideas and innovators across the organization · Connect knowledge, skills, and resources · Build processes to gather, channel, and test new ideas · Link execution and innovating engines	· Create management structure for innovating · Institutionalize norms and values for innovating · Create and legitimize a common language for innovating
Creation	· Constantly look for new ideas that create value for customers and for the organization · Listen to the voice of the customer, the silence of the customer, and learn from noncustomers	· Coach and motivate frontline innovators · Create and manage space for innovating · Make innovating a habit · Review proposed new ideas	· Set time and performance standards for new ideas · Set incentives for innovating behaviors and outcomes for frontline innovators and midlevel coaches

FIGURE A.1 The BTI Framework Expanded

Innovation by Anyone, Anytime, Anywhere—How the Three Processes of Innovating Take Place at Three Levels of an Organization

ACKNOWLEDGMENTS

As any author will tell you, creating a book is not a solo effort. Rather, it reflects the generous help and support of a networks of friends, advisors, influencers, and others who made the author's achievements possible. *Built to Innovate* is no exception. I'm pleased to acknowledge my debt to the following individuals and organizations, without whom this book would never have seen the light of day. Of course, it should be understood that any flaws, errors, or shortcomings that this book may contain are my responsibility alone.

Let me begin by thanking Ilian Mihov, Dean of INSEAD, for his personal support and trust, and for his role in making possible the institutional and financial backing I received from INSEAD. In particular, I am grateful to him in his role as former Dean of Faculty for granting me an essential, highly rewarding sabbatical leave at UC Berkeley, in the heart of Silicon Valley. I am also grateful for the early financial support from the Lucent Technologies research grant to the INSEAD Euro-Asia Centre. In addition, I want to recognize and thank Peter Zemsky, INSEAD Deputy Dean and Dean of Innovation, for his encouragement and trust and for his advocacy, energy, and highly contagious enthusiasm for innovation.

Next, I need to express my appreciation to those whose intellectual influence and support have been important to me. The thinking and insights set forth in the book are the result of my personal intellectual journey and growth, from my years of training as an engineer in France through my graduate studies in Japan and the United States to my years as an educator and researcher at INSEAD, working with stimulating and inspiring colleagues.

First among the three most important intellectual influences that shaped this book are Professor W. Chan Kim and Professor Renée Mauborgne, creators of Blue Ocean Strategy. Starting in 1998, Chan Kim caringly spent long hours with me, patiently explaining his theory and key ideas and training me in teaching Value Innovation and then BOS, which came to make up my second stream of teaching, focused on innovation. He also introduced me to a number of top Blue Ocean Strategy consultants and trainers (see below) who have further deepened my professional knowledge.

Next, I am deeply grateful to the late Professor Sumantra Ghoshal for his personal "open door policy" and the generosity with which he shared his ideas, excitement, and energy. He mentored me during my first teaching period (1992–1997) when I created a new course on the networked organization that included key concepts and examples that would be reflected in the book *The Individualized Corporation* that Ghoshal coauthored with Christopher A. Bartlett.

The third major period in my life that left an important intellectual imprint on me, and the book, is my experience in Japan starting in 1981, with my direct involvement and first-hand observation of Japanese business management style and, in particular, the Japanese view on business process management. I thank Professor Miyakawa for his teaching, insights, and personal caring during my graduate studies at Hitotsubashi University. I also want to express my debt to Professor N. Venkatraman and Professor Michael Scott Morton, who later trained me as a researcher and supervised my PhD dissertation at MIT on the management of supplier relationships by US and Japanese automakers. I am also deeply grateful to Mrs. Yuko Unoki, who facilitated my direct access to Japanese car companies and their C-suites.

My thinking and practice have also been greatly enriched by the network of Value Innovation and Blue Ocean Strategy consultants and experts who shared with me their experience, expertise, and skills, and taught me so much about the art and science of consulting and coaching executives. In particular, I want to mention Marc Beauvois-Coladon, as my partner during our research on NTT DoCoMo i-mode and as my coach during a consulting project with a Singapore government ministry; Jens Meyer and George Eapon, who taught me a lot and, in 2004, codesigned with me the Value Innovation Exploration Workshop (VIEW) for the International Executive Program (IEP), and then the Transition to General Management (TGM) program for Professor and Program Director Michael Pich; Kee-Hian Tan, who supported me in my consulting work with Sabancı group companies, including Kordsa; Ralph Trombetta, who supported me during my teaching and coaching programs with Recruit Holdings in Japan; and Yoshihiko Abe, Jason Hunter, Michael Olenick, Holger Trautmann, and Nana von Bernuth, who all generously shared with me insights from their own consulting and coaching experiences, and provided valuable feedback on early versions of the manuscript.

Many thanks to my academic colleagues for their intellectual stimulation and enrichment, for their continuous guidance, and for the feedback they provided me along the long journey creating this book: Professors Fares Boulos, Jon Chilingerian, James Costantini, Vincent Dominé, Yves Doz, Georges Eapon, Nathan Furr, Charles Galunic, Spencer Harrison, Quy Huy, Michael Jarrett, Neil Jones, Kevin Kaiser, Ji-Yub (Jay) Kim, Jean-Claude Larréché, Marc Le Menestrel, Chengyi Lin, Erin Meyer, Jens Meyer, Phil Parker, Loïc Sadoulet, José Santos, Michael Shiel, James Teboul, Ludo Van der Heyden, N. Venkatraman, David Young, and Peter Zemsky. Special thanks to Jon Chilingerian, Charles Galunic, and Quy Huy for their insightful suggestions on different versions of the manuscript.

A crucial role in the creation of *Built to Innovate* was played by the hundreds of company executives who helped with the research, made time to describe their practices, and opened their offices and facilities for me to observe and interview their teams. Many of them also accepted my invitation to be featured in the book. Those I wish to thank include the following:

- ▶ Cenk Alper (Kordsa and Sabancı Group)
- ▶ Christian Bachler and Mika Sokka (Fiskars)
- ▶ Jan Carendi, Tony Benitez, Veit Stutz, and Pramod Arikal (Allianz)
- ▶ Naoji Iwashita (Recruit Holdings)
- ▶ Andrés Jaffé and Uwe Hartwig (BASF)
- ▶ Monika Lessl and Henning Trill (Bayer)
- ▶ Donal O'Riain and Maria Beloso Hall (Ecocem)
- ▶ Robyn Pratt and Renaud Lamoureux (Starwood)
- ▶ Judith Werkman-Loenen and Klaas Kruithoff (AkzoNobel)

Thanks are also due to the thousands of MBA, EMBA, and executive participants I have had the pleasure and privilege of teaching over the last 20 years. It has been deeply gratifying for me to see many of these executives pursue and implement the ideas, processes, and tools I've shared with them in classes and training sessions, stay in touch with me, and provide inspiring feedback. It is a confirmation that executive education can have a meaningful long-term impact and significant return on investment for clients. I want to give a special mention to the first executives who went through the VIEW workshops I conducted in IEP and TGM programs early in my teaching period focused on innovation. I also want to recognize the late Professor Michael Pich, who first invited me to offer the VIEW workshops as part of his IEP and TGM programs. My appreciation also goes to Professor Michael Jarrett and Professor James Teboul for inviting me to teach in their programs for Fiskars and Starwood, respectively.

Thanks to my literary agent, Tom Miller of Liza Dawson Associates, and to the members of the McGraw Hill team who supported me with great professionalism, especially my editor Stephen Isaacs.

My authorship partner Karl Weber helped me in ways that extended beyond the obvious tasks of writing and editing the text. He also suggested ideas and case studies, supported the research effort, and joined me in recent years in visiting some of the companies we profiled and interviewing their executives. I'm grateful for Karl's help in making this book better. Karl's contribution, both intellectual and emotional, deserves a special mention as an integral part of this book. Thank you, Karl!

Finally, and most important, I need to thank those in my life who are closest to me: my wife, Masako, and our three sons, Sophian, Alexis, and Lennon. The love we share inspires all my efforts to learn and grow as a thinker, a professional, and a human being.

Ben M. Bensaou
Fontainebleau, France

NOTES

Introduction

1. The three-by-three BTI framework depicted in Figure I.1 is adapted from a similar model presented by Sumantra Ghoshal and Christopher A. Bartlett in their book *The Individualized Corporation: A Fundamentally New Approach to Management* (London: Heinemann, 1998). An expanded version of the BTI framework appears in the Appendix.

2. The term *collective genius* is most often associated with the work of Professor Linda A. Hill of the Harvard Business School, especially her book *Collective Genius: The Art and Practice of Leading Innovation* (Harvard Business Review Press, 2014), coauthored with Greg Brandeau, Emily Truelove, and Kent Lineback.

Chapter 1: The Innovating Habit

1. On the Haber-Bosch process, see Claudia Flavell-While, "Fritz Haber and Carl Bosch—Feed the World," *The Chemical Engineer,* March 2, 2010, https://www.thechemicalengineer.com/features/cewctw-fritz-haber-and-carl-bosch-feed-the-world/.

2. The insights into BASF's innovating methods in this chapter are drawn in part from author interviews with Andrés Jaffé, head of Perspectives, and members of the Perspectives team on March 17, 2009; April 22–24, 2009; and May 5, 2010; and author interviews with Dr. Uwe Hartwig, senior vice president, Perspectives, May 20, 2016, and Michael-Georg Schmidt, director, Perspectives, October 11, 2016, and February 9, 2021.

3. "Designing Customer Centricity for Multiple Market Segments: The *Perspectives* Project," in *Designing the Smart Organization: How*

Breakthrough Corporate Learning Initiatives Drive Strategic Change and Innovation by Roland Deiser (Pfeiffer, 2009).

4. "Total silence at the Guggenheim Museum through BASF's foam Basotect," BASF news release, April 5, 2017, https://www.basf.com /global/en/media/news-releases/2017/04/p-17-180.html.

5. Quotations in the two previous paragraphs from "Business model innovation—the sky is the limit!" Set of business model cards edited by Christian Huber of BASF Perspectives, March 2015.

Chapter 2: Execution and Innovating

1. Charles A. O'Reilly III and Michael L. Tushman, "The Ambidextrous Organization," *Harvard Business Review*, April 2004.

2. Vijay Govindarajan and Srikanth Srinavas, "The Innovative Mindset in Action: 3M Corporation," *Harvard Business Review,* August 6, 2013.

3. Thanks to Frédéric Amariutei of W. L. Gore for helping me understand how the core values and guiding principles originally set forth by Bill and Vieve Gore continue to shape the company's innovating engine today.

4. Gary Hamel, "Innovation Democracy: W.L. Gore's Original Management Model," Management Innovation eXchange, September 23, 2010.

5. Simon Caulkin, "W.L. Gore: the company others try and fail to imitate," *Financial Times*, August 2, 2019.

6. Adam M. Brandenburger and Harborne W. Stuart, Jr., "Value-Based Business Strategy," *MIT Journal of Economics & Management Strategy,* Spring, 1996, pages 5–24.

7. Moon Ihlwan, "Camp Samsung," *Bloomberg Businessweek*, July 2, 2006.

8. Jeremy Horwitz, "Apple's By Innovation Only event established Samsung as the trailblazer," *Beat*, September 11, 2019.

9. Haydn Shaughnessey, "What Makes Samsung Such an Innovative Company?," *Forbes,* March 7, 2013.

10. SeHo Cheong, "TRIZ experiences at SMD," slide presentation, March 21, 2011, https://www.osaka-gu.ac.jp/php/nakagawa /TRIZ/eTRIZ/epapers/e2011Papers/eSHCheongTRIZSymp2010 /eSHCheong-TRIZSymp2010-110917.htm.

11. See Son Wook, "Value Innovation and Goal-Oriented Management Made Samsung TV "The Global No. 1,'" *Hankyung Business,* December 21, 2011.

12. Moon Ihlwan, "Camp Samsung."

13. Daniel Saunders, "How Samsung stays one step ahead in the innovation race," *Qualtrics* website, February 26, 2020.

14. I'm indebted for this insight, among others, to Dr. Chang Sea-Jin, the Lim Kim San Chair Professor of Business Administration at National University of Singapore (NUS) Business School and author of *Sony vs. Samsung: The Inside Story of the Electronics Giants' Battle for Global Supremacy* (Wiley, 2008).

15. See, for example, Asad Zaidi, "Brainstorming Using the Walt Disney Method," *Management Insights,* October 10, 2019, http://mdi .com.pk/management/2019/10/brainstorming-using-the-walt-disney -method/.

Chapter 3: The Innovating Perspective

1. Whitney Wetsig, "Scientists and engineers train like warfighters during annual Operation Tech Warrior event," Wright-Patterson AFB website, October 18, 2018.

2. "Small Businesses Participate in Air Force SBIR/STTR Tech Warrior Enterprise Event," Federal Laboratory Consortium for Technology Transfer website, May 16, 2018, https://federallabs.org/news/small -businesses-participate-in-air-force-sbirsttr-tech-warrior-enterprise -event.

3. The insights into Ecocem's innovating methods in this chapter are drawn in part from author interviews with Donal O'Riain, founder and managing director of Ecocem Materials Limited, November 11, 2020, and November 24, 2020, and with behavioral transformation and change management coach Maria Beloso Hall, March 11, 2021.

4. Kraig Becker, "Gore's Innovation Center Is a Powerful Ally for Silicon Valley Startups," *DigitalTrends*, April 6, 2019.

5. Information on AkzoNobel's Paint the Future program is drawn in part from author interviews with Klaas Kruithof, chief technology officer for AkzoNobel, and Judith Werkman-Loenen, director of innovation excellence and sustainability for AkzoNobel, January

28, 2021, and March 1, 2021, as well as from innovation training programs at AkzoNobel led by the author in 2009, 2010, 2012, and 2013.

6. David Gelles, "A Charity Accepts Uber Stock as Donations. Then Uses It to Pay Staff Bonuses. Is That O.K.?" *New York Times,* April 13, 2019.

Chapter 4: The Three Processes of Innovating

1. The insights into innovation at Kordsa and the Sabancı Group in this chapter are drawn in part from author interviews with Mehmet Pekarun, member of the executive committee, the Sabancı Group, October 31, 2016; a series of interviews with Cenk Alper, formerly CTO and CEO of Kordsa and now CEO and a board member of Sabancı Holding, from December 17, 2008, to February 17, 2021; and interviews with Ibrahum Yildirim, chief technology officer, Kordsa; Emel Eren, R&D laboratory leader, Kordsa, October 27, 2016; Burak Turgut Orhun, head of strategy and business development, Sabancı Holding, and Can Ornekol, ventures investment associate, Sabancı Holding, March 4, 2021; Müge Yenmez, market development group manager, Kordsa, March 2, 2021; and Uğur Gülen, general manager, Aksigorta, and Esra Öge, assistant general manager, strategy & transformation, Aksigorta, March 2, 2021. Further insights were drawn from author plant visits, innovation training programs, and project coaching activities in 2006, 2007, 2008, and 2010.

2. Aaron E. Carroll, "The Quiet Research That Led to a Resounding Success in Diabetes Prevention," *New York Times,* March 30, 2016.

3. Paul Barr, "Taking on diabetes: Proven prevention methods get payers' attention," *Modern Healthcare,* December 15, 2012.

4. "Spotlight on Innovation: YMCA's Efforts to Fight Chronic Disease," Better Medicare Alliance website, December 3, 2015, https://www .bettermedicarealliance.org/publication/spotlight-on-innovation -ymcas-efforts-to-fight-chronic-disease/.

5. "After 20-year increase, New Diabetes Cases Decline," CDC press release, May 18, 2019, https://www.cdc.gov/media/releases/2019 /p0529-diabetes-cases-decline.html.

Chapter 5: Anyone, Anytime, Anywhere

1. The insights into innovating at Fiskars in this chapter are drawn in part from author interviews with Thomas Enckell, president of Fiskars, Europe, January 12, 2016; Kari Kauniskangas, CEO, Fiskars Corporation, May 17, 2016; Jari Skyttä, new business manager, Fiskars Brand Finland, May 17, 2016; Jari Ikaheimonen, business line manager, Plant Care, Europe and Asia-Pacific, May 17, 2016; Christian Bachler, business director, Kitchen, May 17, 2016, and February 10, 2021; Pasi Engblom, business director, Garden Europe & Asia Pacific, May 16, 2016; Mika Sokka, Fiskars director of New Product Development, May 18, 2016, June 30, 2016, March 13, 2020, and February 17, 2021; Masalin (Pepe) Petteri, vice president, Design Functional Products, May 18, 2016, and March 2, 2021; and Oliver Zehme, director, Go-To-Market Europe, June 28, 2016. Other insights were drawn from innovation training programs at Fiskars led by the author in 2011 and 2012.

2. "Red Dot: Design Team of the Year 2020," Red Dot website, https://www.red-dot.org/about-red-dot/magazine/fiskars-red-dot-design-team-of-the-year-2020-creates-the-extraordinary-through-tradition-innovation-and-curiosity.

3. Sarah Kessler, "48 Years Later, This Is How Fiskars Keeps Improving On Its Classic Orange-Handled Scissors," *Fast Company,* January 26, 2015, https://www.fastcompany.com/3040816/48-years-later-this-is-how-fiskars-keeps-improving-on-its-classic-orang.

4. Since the interview when Christian Bachler offered that memorable comment, he has risen in the organization to become a member of Fiskars' group leadership team and the executive vice president of Vita, one of the company's three main business divisions.

5. "Fiskars Group sets its sights on circular economy," Fiskars press release, March 18, 2019, https://www.fiskarsgroup.com/media/press-releases/fiskars-group-sets-its-sights-circular-economy-vintage-buy-and-sell-previously.

6. "The Vintage service expands to all Iittala stores in Finland and extends recycling to other manufacturers' broken tableware," Fiskars press release, July 30, 2019, https://news.cision.com/fiskars-release-archive/r/the-vintage-service-expands-to-all-iittala-stores-in-finland-and-extends-recycling-to-other-manufact,c2861483.

Chapter 6: Hands-On Creativity

1. Interview with Stephanos George Eapon, Innomantra Consulting, February 26, 2021.
2. Caroline Baldwin, "How Starwood Hotels is using technology to innovate hospitality," *Essential Retail,* April 14, 2016.
3. Mark R. Vondrasek, "Redefining service innovation at Starwood," *McKinsey Quarterly,* February 1, 2015.
4. Debbie Carson, "Marriott International Commits to Continued Innovation in Hotel Guest-facing Technologies," *Hotel Business Week,* July 9, 2019.
5. *Joy, Inc.: How We Built a Workplace People Love* (Porfolio, 2015).
6. Quoted in "Valve's Way," by Phanish Puranam and Dorthe Døjbak Häkonsson, *Journal of Organization Design,* June 23, 2015.
7. "A Lesson from Valve on The Importance of Innovation," by Sudarshan Gopaladesikan, Gamification.co, May 10, 2013.
8. *Valve Handbook for New Employees: A fearless adventure in knowing what to do when there's no one there telling you what to do* (Valve Press, 2012). Online at https://cdn.cloudflare.steamstatic.com/apps/valve /Valve_NewEmployeeHandbook.pdf.
9. Ryan Cooper, "How capitalism killed one of the best video game studios," *The Week,* June 4, 2019.
10. Reed Hastings and Erin Meyer, *No Rules Rules: Netflix and the Culture of Reinvention* (Penguin Press, 2020).

Chapter 7: Coaching Innovation

1. The insights into innovating at Allianz and some of the details concerning the *i2s* program came from author interviews with Jan Carendi, CEO, Allianz of Americas, head of the NAFTA region/ Latin America, and member of the Board of Management, March 26, 2007; Dr. Werner Zedelius, head of growth markets and member of the Board of Management, November 11, 2008; Cameron Pearson, general manager, Growth Innovation & Marketing, Mondial Assistance, January 26, 2009, and August 26, 2010; Pramod Arikal, head, International Business, Syncier (B2B2X Insurtech Allianz subsidiary company), February 16, 2021; and Veit Stutz, formerly head of *i2S* and now global head of business transformation, Allianz,

March 12, 2021. Further information was provided by interviews with 16 members of AGO unit (Allianz Group OPEX) and a member of Group Economic Research and Corporate Development, between March 19, 2009, and May 17, 2010, as well as communication with Helen Williams, head of organizational change and capability building, Allianz (email exchange dated March 21, 2021).

2. Hind Benbya and Dorothy Leidner, "Harnessing Employee Innovation in Idea Management Platforms: Lessons from Allianz UK," *MIS Quarterly Executive,* October 2017.

3. Ibid.

4. Kenny MacIver, "Allianz: Enriching customer experience through digitalization," *Global Intelligence for Digital Leaders,* June 2016.

5. Adlina A. Rahim, "How Allianz is digitizing to keep up with today's insurtech players," *Techwire Asia,* March 13, 2020.

6. Caroline Poser, "Allianz created an AI-powered virtual assistant," *IBM Case Studies,* https://www.ibm.com/case-studies/allianz-taiwan -life-insurance/.

7. Interview with Pramod Arikal, head of international business at Syncier, which provides digital service solutions to Allianz and other insurance clients, February 16, 2021.

8. Jeff John Roberts, "IBM received the most patents in 2020. Here's the rest of the top 20," *Fortune,* January 21, 2021, https://fortune .com/2021/01/12/ibm-most-patents-2020-full-rankings/.

9. Greg Satell, "How IBM Innovates," *Forbes,* January 19, 2016, https:// www.forbes.com/sites/gregsatell/2016/01/19/how-ibm-innovates/?sh =743f8a897f60.

10. Kristof Kloeckner, "Building an Enterprise Culture of Continuous Innovation," *Forbes Technology Council,* April 9, 2019, https:// www.forbes.com/sites/forbestechcouncil/2018/04/09/building-an -enterprise-culture-of-continuous-innovation/?sh=102a588d6824/.

11. See Charles A. O'Reilly III and Michael L. Tushman, *Lead and Disrupt: How to Solve the Innovator's Dilemma,* Chapter 5 (Stanford, 2016).

12. The insights into innovation at Recruit in this chapter are drawn in part from author interviews and research visits that began in August 2002 and extended to April 2021, when the author exchanged messages with the Recruit Business Competence Institute. Additional

insights are drawn from author interviews with Naoji Iwashita, then executive manager, CarSensor, and visits to car dealerships, November 18, 2002, and from innovation training programs led by the author, August and November 2002.

13. Sandra J. Sucher and Shalene Gupta, "Globalizing Japan's Dream Machine: Recruit Holdings Co., Ltd." Harvard Business School case, April 25, 2018.

14. Howard Yu, "My views on Recruit," Recruit Holdings website, https://recruit-holdings.com/who/value/post_36.html.

15. The story of B-MATCH was shared with the author by the Recruit Business Competence Institute in a memo titled "Innovation at Recruit Group," August 18, 2020, and in an email message with updates provided by Masami Muro and Ryo Maeda, April 19, 2021.

Chapter 8: Setting the Agenda

1. "Jonathan Becher, Chief Digital Officer, SAP," Conversations with Top Innovators, June 28, 2013, https://www.cxotalk.com/episode /jonathan-becher-chief-digital-officer-sap.

2. Erik Charles, "Sales Disruptors: How San Jose Sharks President Jonathan Becher Is Innovating the Fan Experience Despite the COVID-19 Pandemic," podcast on MarketScale website, June 19, 2020, https://marketscale.com/industries/software-and-technology /how-san-jose-sharks-president-jonathan-becher-is-innovating-the -fan-experience-despite-the-covid-19-pandemic/.

3. Michael Krigsman, "San Jose Sharks: Fan experience, community, and technology (but don't call it digital transformation)," Beyond IT Failure, ZDNet.com, October 22, 2018.

4. Paul Greenberg, "Engaging fans during a pandemic: How the San Jose Sharks simulate hockey games," Social CRM: The Conversation, August 24, 2020.

5. Ibid.

6. The insights into Ecocem's innovating methods in this chapter are drawn in part from author interviews with Donal O'Riain, founder and managing director of Ecocem Materials Limited, November 11, 2020, and November 24, 2020, and with behavioral transformation and change management coach Maria Beloso Hall, March 11, 2021.

7. Interview with Stephanos George Eapon, Innomantra Consulting, February 26, 2021.

Chapter 9: Igniting the Engine

1. The insights into Bayer's innovating methods in this chapter are drawn in part from author interviews with Dr. Monika Lessl, senior vice president and head of corporate innovation, R&D, and social innovation at Bayer AG, and Dr. Henning Trill, vice president of innovation strategy, Bayer AG, conducted on May 11, 2020, June 30, 2020, and August 21, 2020.
2. "Big Pharma, Big Changes: How Bayer and Johnson & Johnson Innovate," *Innov8ers News,* March 12, 2018, https://innov8rs.co /news/big-pharma-big-changes-bayer-johnson-johnson-innovate/.
3. Ibid.
4. Interview with Burak Turgut Orhun, head of strategy and business development, Sabancı Holding, March 6, 2021.
5. Interview with Tomas Granlund, vice president of new business development, Fiskars Group, March 2, 2021.
6. Monika Lessl, Henning Trill, and Julian Birkinshaw, "Fostering Employee Innovation at a 150-Year-Old Company," *Harvard Business Review,* December 17, 2018.

Chapter 10: Priming the Pump

1. Spencer Harrison, Arne Carlsen, and Miha Skerlavaj, "Marvel's Blockbuster Machine," *Harvard Business Review,* July–August 2019.
2. "List of highest-grossing superhero films," Wikipedia, accessed January 30, 2021.
3. Amit Agnihotri, "Why Innovate? 3 Lessons from Avengers: Endgame," Why Innovation website, December 2020, https://www.why -innovation.com/why-innovate-3-lessons-from-avengers:-endgame.
4. W. Chan Kim and Renée Mauborgne, *Blue Ocean Strategy: How to Create Uncontested Market Space and Make the Competition Irrelevant* (Harvard Business Review Press, 2005); *Blue Ocean Shift: Beyond Competing—Proven Steps to Inspire Confidence and Seize New Growth* (Hachette, 2017).

5. Thomas Lockwood, *Design Thinking: Integrating Innovation, Customer Experience and Brand Value* (Allworth, 2010); Vijay Kumar, *101 Design Methods: A Structured Approach for Driving Innovation in Your Organization* (Wiley, 2012).

6. The six preconditions listed here have been inspired by the work on fair process leadership and high-performance teams by Ludo Van der Heyden, professor of Technology and Operations Management at INSEAD and the INSEAD Chaired Professor in Corporate Governance.

7. Tom Kelley and David Kelley, "Why Designers Should Never Go to a Meeting Without a Prototype," *Slate*, October 23, 2013, https://slate.com/human-interest/2013/10/the-importance-of-prototyping -creative-confidence-by-tom-and-david-kelley.html.

8. A detailed examination of Marvel Studios' business transformation is found in "The Marvel Way: Restoring a Blue Ocean," a business case written by Michael Olenick under the supervision of W. Chan Kim and Renée Mauborgne (INSEAD Blue Ocean Strategy Institute, 2016), https://store.hbr.org/product/the-marvel-way-restoring-a-blue -ocean/IN1182.

9. Spencer Harrison, "Marvel's Blockbuster Machine."

10. Ibid.

11. "Most Innovative Companies: Marvel Studios," *Fast Company*, https://www.fastcompany.com/company/marvel-studios.

12. Spencer Harrison, "Marvel's Blockbuster Machine."

Chapter 11: Keeping the Engine Humming

1. Giselle Abramovich, "Domino's CDO Shares His Secret Sauce For Innovation," CMO.com, April 18,2018.

2. Ibid.

3. Ibid.

4. Nancy Luna, "Domino's tech leaders reveal 3 big innovations coming soon," *Nation's Restaurant News,* October 23, 2019.

5. Trung T. Phan, "Domino's has been working on pizza delivery innovation for years. During quarantine, its efforts have paid off," *The Hustle*, September 21, 2020.

6. Brian Solis, "Domino's Pizza Serves Up Innovations In Customer Experience (CX) To Drive Business Growth," CMO Network, August 15, 2018.

7. *Fast Company,* "Most Innovative Companies: Top 50, Branding," 2019, https://www.fastcompany.com/company/dominos.

8. Jonathan Maze, "Domino's Works to Keep Its Technology Edge," *Restaurant Business*, October 25, 2019.

9. Ibid.

10. Frank Witsil, "How Domino's used technology to woo millennials and beat rival Pizza Hut," *Detroit Free Press,* March 6, 2018.

11. *Fast Company,* "Most Innovative Companies."

12. Isabelle Gustafson, "Domino's Opens 'Innovation Garage' to Test New Technology," *CStore Decisions,* September 3, 2019.

13. Giselle Abramovich, "Domino's CDO."

14. Jonathan Maze, "Domino's Works to Keep Its Technology Edge."

15. Anna Wolfe, "Is Contactless Delivery Here to Stay?," *Hospitality Technology,* May 11, 2020.

16. Seth Stevenson, "What It's Like to Deliver Pizza in a Pandemic," *Slate*, June 30, 2020.

INDEX

ABOUT THE AUTHOR

Ben M. Bensaou is Professor of Technology Management and Professor of Asian Business and Comparative Management at INSEAD, Fontainebleau, France. He served as Dean of Executive Education in 2018–2020. He was a Visiting Associate Professor at the Harvard Business School for 1998–1999, a Senior Fellow at the Wharton School of Management for 2007–2008, and a Visiting Scholar at the Haas School of Business at UC Berkeley for 2013–2015.

He holds a PhD in Management from MIT Sloan School of Management, Cambridge, USA, an MA in Management Science from Hitotsubashi University, Tokyo, Japan, a Diplôme d'Ingénieur (MS) in Civil Engineering, and a Diplôme d'Études Approfondies (DEA) in Mechanical Engineering from two Grandes Écoles in France: the École Nationale des Travaux Publics de l'État, Lyon, and the Institut National Polytechnique de Grenoble.

Bensaou's research and teaching activities focus on (1) how to create innovating capabilities and competencies as a way to build an innovating organization and culture; (2) Blue Ocean Strategy and Value Innovation implementation and roll-out processes across the whole organization; (3) how to build social capital within firms; (4) new forms of organizations, in particular, networked corporations, strategic alliances, joint ventures, and value-adding partnerships; and (5) the impact of digital technologies on innovation. He addresses these issues from an international comparative perspective, with a special focus on Japanese organizations.

Bensaou's research on buyer–supplier relations in the US and Japanese auto industries won him the Best Doctoral Dissertation Award in the field of information systems and a finalist honor in the Free Press Award competition for outstanding dissertation research in the field of business policy and strategy. His cases on Innovation won him multiple Best Case Awards at The Case Centre. His publications include papers in *Academy of Management Journal, Management Science, Information Systems Research, Organization Science, Strategic Management Journal, the Journal of International Business Studies, Harvard Business Review, Sloan Management Review*, book chapters, and conference proceedings. He has been a member of the Editorial Board of *Information Systems Research, MIS Quarterly* and *MISQ Executive*.